"Mind control is so fi... t thing one can do is learn the tr... that in the most comprehensive examination of the .... From its pervasive use in media and marketing, to being one of the darkest tools of the nefarious Elite. If knowledge is power, then *Mind Wars* is mind control Kryptonite!"

—Greg Carlwood, host of conspiracy podcast,
The Higherside Chats

"For those who think that the desire to control and know what you think at all times is a new phenomena...think again! In their latest book, Marie D. Jones and Larry Flaxman show that throughout history powers and principalities have spied, manipulated and otherwise attempted to discern what we think in order to harness the power of our minds. What is even scarier is what lies ahead! Within a few short years, will technology render the concept of a private thought obsolete? What evil could be done with this tremendous power? You'll have to read *Mind Wars* to find out. Don't just think about it, buy this book today before THEY say you can't!"

—Jim Harold, president, Jim Harold Media LLC;
host of the Paranormal Podcast and Jim Harold's Campfire;
author of *Jim Harold's Campfire: True Ghost Stories* and
True Ghost Stories: Jim Harold's Campfire 2

MIND
WARS

A History of Mind Control, Surveillance, and Social Engineering by the Government, Media, and Secret Societies

MARIE D. JONES
AND
LARRY FLAXMAN

New Page Books
A Division of The Career Press, Inc.
Pompton Plains, NJ

MIND WARS
EDITED BY JODI BRANDON
TYPESET BY GINA SCHENCK
Cover design by Brian Moore
Printed in the U.S.A.

To order this title, please call toll-free 1-800-CAREER-1 (NJ and Canada: 201-848-0310) to order using VISA or MasterCard, or for further information on books from Career Press.

The Career Press, Inc.
220 West Parkway, Unit 12
Pompton Plains, NJ 07444
www.careerpress.com
www.newpagebooks.com

Library of Congress Cataloging-in-Publication Data

CIP Data Available Upon Request.

To Mary Essa and Max

ACKNOWLEDGMENTS

Marie and Larry would like to thank Lisa Hagan, agent extraordinaire, for always championing our work and being a good friend in the process. You are the best! We would also like to thank Michael Pye and the team at New Page Books for their ongoing belief in our vision and work, and to Warwick Associates for their wonderful work publicizing our books to the world. And to our readers and all those who hosted us on their radio shows and at events, thank you so much. Without you, we are nothing. A huge thank you to Ron Patton, Editor-in-Chief of Paranoia Magazine, for your input, direction, and research! Thank you also to everyone who contributed to this book. Your input and insights made it so much richer and we so appreciate you all.

Larry

I would like to express my gratitude to the many people who were instrumental in helping to make this book possible. First, I'd like to thank my mom and dad, whose boundless love, teachings, and ethos will remain with me forever. I would give anything to travel back in time and relive all of the moments where I thought that I knew better. I know that we will be reunited one day, and look forward to the opportunity to listen and learn again. Without both of you, I would not be here writing these words.

Thanks to my wife, Emily, for putting up with me and all of my "eccentricities." You are a wonderful mother, inspiration, and friend. Without your seemingly endless amount of patience and understanding I would never have had the ability to follow my dreams.

I want to give a special thanks to my partner in crime, Marie D. Jones. Through the good, the bad, the thick, and the thin, we have stuck together and put out some phenomenal books. While things haven't always been easy, our common goals have remained steadfast. Thank you for always pushing me to fuel my own inner fire. You have provided inspiration beyond measure. Here's to another six and beyond!

I would be remiss if I forgot to thank our wonderful publisher: New Page Books. Thank you for believing in Marie and me enough to publish six of our books. You guys have been great to work with and we look forward to the future!

A special thanks to all of my friends, fans, and even critics that I have met while on this journey. All of you help to keep me grounded and "real."

Finally, and most importantly. A special thank you to my daughter, Mary Essa (aka "The Honey"). You are truly the wind beneath my wings. Every time I look at you I see absolute perfection. I would never in a million years have believed that this level of love would be possible. I am so incredibly proud of you and I look forward to a lifetime of adventure, exploration, and learning together.

Marie

I would like to thank my mom, Milly, who is the best mom on the planet hands down and still takes good care of me; my brother, John; and my dad, John, who is up there in heaven cheering me on. My family rocks and they are always there for me! To my sister and best friend, Angella, who is my rock and keeps me sane—sort of! Thank you for everything!!! You are my hero with your courage and ability to overcome huge challenges and stay snarky and wonderful!

I would like to thank everyone who has reached out to me about these books or listened to me on radio, and I am so grateful for everyone who takes the time to read what I write and contact me. My dear friends and colleagues, you all keep me inspired and motivated more than I can ever express. Lisa Hagan, what can I say? We just make such a great team and I love you dearly! We go wayyyy back!

Ron Patton, this book would not exist without your support, suggestions, expertise, and help, and I owe you so much for helping to research and contact experts and keep the book on the right track. Your friendship and belief in me and in this book are priceless and something I will never forget. Thank you for being there.

Larry Flaxman, wow—seven years and…how many books and articles and radio shows and events? How many e-mails and texts and messages and phone calls? I lost track a long time ago, but I am eternally grateful for your constant presence in my life and for having you as a partner and a friend. We've certainly had our share of rough times, and yet, we still manage to pull through and "get 'er done," and I think that is a testament to the deep bond we created all those years ago when we said, "Hey, let's form an alliance." Some of the best conversations of my life have been us on the phone for hours going back and forth about some paranormal or scientific theory (which eventually turned into books!). Here's to a whole new direction and another seven years or more!

And most of all, to my heart and my soul, my universe, my sun and moon and stars—Max. Without you, there is no point to any of this. I hope I make you proud. You make me proud. You, my son, are my hero.

Contents

Authors' Note

This is a difficult subject to write about. So much exists in the way of allegations, anecdotal evidence, assumptions, conspiracies, and theories, not to mention the factual and statistical, and we would be remiss to leave any of this material out of a comprehensive look at mind control and surveillance. However, we as authors have this little thing that publishers impose upon us called "word count," and we are forced to leave out many topics and tangents that readers might be interested in, and cut short many subjects we could have, with a massive word count, gone fully in depth on. That is just the way of the world in book publishing. We did our best to touch upon the key elements, introducing them and adding depth when we possibly could, and we always welcome readers to expand their own knowledge by taking the trip down the rabbit hole on their own. We also wish to express that not all of the ideas and theories presented in this book are ones we or our publisher agree with, but if authors only wrote about the stuff they agreed with, books would cease to exist—or be awfully boring. We hope that in the space we were given, we have presented enough solid material and intriguing theory to create a strong sense of curiosity and desire for increased knowledge in you, the reader. This is serious stuff. Knowledge is power. And the mind truly is a terrible thing to waste.

Use yours wisely.

INTRODUCTION

From the dawn of humanity, the desire to control the thoughts, behaviors, and actions of others has been a pervasive one. But few people know that mind control techniques have been around since the beginning of civilization itself. As long as we were aware that we had separate minds and thought processes, we were also aware of the desire to control the minds and thought processes of others, for whatever motive or gain. It may have stemmed from a desire to simply understand if others thought as we did, or to know what the enemy was planning, or whether a suitor was, well, suited to our tastes or not. As with the apple in the Garden of Eden, which gave Adam and Eve knowledge they were not supposed to have, the moment we gained the knowledge of our differences of opinions and beliefs and traditions and ideas, we opened up a Pandora's box that could never be contained or closed again.

From the use of coercive persuasion by ancient Egyptians and the Knights Templar, to the mass mind manipulations and torture utilized by political and religious authorities through the Dark and Middle Ages, to World War II and the inhumane Nazi experimentation on concentration camp prisoners, to the more recent CIA's Project MKUltra (now declassified) mind control programs of the 1950s and the trauma-based Project Monarch, to today's claims of gang-stalking, electronic harassment, microwave "bombing" and neuro-linguistic programming (NLP), we have been victims of those who wish to hack into the privacy of the mind's computer and rewrite our very thoughts and beliefs. These "handlers" and "programmers" desire to reshape the mind into weapons of war and assassination, using either trauma-based or electronic-based intrusions, sometimes coupled with ritual abuse, occult practices, and even mutilation and torture.

Our past has hidden deep, dark secrets.

Mind Wars will present a comprehensive history of the past, present, and future of mind control, and electronic surveillance and harassment, as well as the more insidious influences of cults, politics, religion, and the media in the creation and influence of mass thought and manipulation. From the ad agencies that use subliminal imagery to the preachers and politicians who use NLP to the ubiquitous themes and motifs found in mass media and entertainment, mind control doesn't just occur in top-secret military installations or in the basements of major universities. It happens every day to each and every one of us.

But the real story of mind control is about the highly classified use of often-torturous and always-invasive methods conducted on innocent victims and human guinea pigs in the quest to create submission and obedience, as well as the most insidious and futuristic invasions into the deepest recesses of our minds, where we think we have sovereignty over our reality.

The goal of *Mind Wars* is to present an objective and comprehensive examination of mind control and other forms of covert harassment aimed at controlling individual and collective behavior: what we know, what is alleged, what people claim to have first-hand experience of. There are conspiracies galore when it comes to these subjects, and oftentimes just wading through the fiction from the fact is exhausting and mazelike, because those involved are not used to being direct, open, and truthful. That is the power of the manipulation of the mind—to keep one guessing and confused, and to prevent clarity because in clarity there is truth.

As much as we hate to admit it, there are people and institutions that will do just about anything to not let us be of clear mind enough to see that truth.

Yet at the same time, we authors must admit we had no idea of the sheer amount of research that exists about these subjects, and we only had a certain number of pages we were allowed to fill, which has forced us to choose to touch upon many subjects, without being able to go deeper down the rabbit hole. We leave that to you, readers. Our hope is that we touched upon as many of the most critical topics as we could and presented a powerful introduction to what we hope will spur further inquiry. Mind control alone could fill 10 books; surveillance another 10. But we hope this book is a good start along the path of knowledge, empowerment, and discovery. In addition, we strongly encourage you, dear reader, to visit the sources mentioned and quoted throughout the book, as well as the sources in our Bibliography for more detailed examinations of so many of the topics we barely scratched the surface of.

The quest to achieve the ultimate power of controlling the human mind continues with the most cutting-edge discoveries and research, which we will document, into ways to alter, shape, and create false memories, altered realities, and manipulated perceptions, including potential technology that will one day read our thoughts before we even think them. The future is downright scary unless we can find ways to protect the sanctity of our inner realities, our minds and our awareness, and our ability to choose and decide what is right and wrong, up and down.

Lest you, dear reader, think that mind control is a thing of the past, or an overused subject of sci-fi movies and thrillers starring Frank Sinatra or Mel Gibson, it is alive and well and coming to a theater of the mind near you—maybe even playing directly on *your* screen.

The human mind is the last bastion of privacy, where we can be who we are, think what we want, and behave in accordance with our values and beliefs. But the pervasive presence of mind control and mental manipulation threatens to take away that basic and fundamental human right—the right to own our own mind.

1

(KEEP ON PLAYING THOSE) MIND GAMES: MIND CONTROL FOR THE MASSES

Brainwashing is a system of befogging the brain so a person can be seduced into acceptance of what otherwise would be abhorrent to him. He loses touch with reality. Facts and fancy whirl round and change places....
—Edward Hunter, *Brainwashing*

The most dangerous of all sciences is that of molding mass opinion, because it would enable anyone to govern the whole world.
—Talbot Mundy

In a world that leaves little to the imagination, where everything from our bodies to our sex lives is readily available for all to see via the new reality of social networking, where what we had for dinner and who we are divorcing becomes global information for whoever has the time and the inclination to care, where our photos and posts and e-mails are being perused not only by family and friends and colleagues, but secretive government agencies, we are as transparent as Saran Wrap. Yet, perhaps naively, we believe that the inner sanctum of the mind is our last bastion of privacy, where our most deepest, darkest secrets can remain buried in shadows, and our hopes and dreams and how we really feel about our mother-in-law or boss will never see the light of day (unless we choose to post it on our social networking!). The mind, to us, is ours and ours alone, and even our closest loved ones only get to know what we choose to share with them.

We and we alone control our behaviors, think our thoughts, plan our actions, and express our emotions, as autonomous beings in a conform-crazy world.

Our minds are *our* minds.

Yet from the beginning of time, others have desired to make us think, believe, and behave according to *their* minds, and the desire to control the most private and powerful part of our identity was a Golden Fleece, a Holy Grail, to those whom, for whatever motive or purpose, would benefit from being the puppet-master to our puppet.

Mind control is probably as old as our awareness that we each had a mind of our own.

Throughout the course of history, there are a number of names for mind control that describe a common goal: to take over a person's inner-most thoughts and control his or her behaviors and actions. Brainwashing, coercion, thought reform, mental manipulation, psychological warfare, programming, conversion, gas lighting, indoctrination methods, psychic driving, crowd control: They all describe a method by which a person's individual thoughts, beliefs, and perceptions are disrupted, dismissed, and destroyed—even replaced with the thoughts, beliefs, and perceptions of someone else. Whether designed to create the perfect assassin or super soldier, indoctrinate prisoners of war, recruit members into a cult or religious belief system, or control the consuming masses and direct their behaviors in accordance to the political whims of the day, mind control has been used extensively in our past, is in use today, and no doubt will be used in the future.

And lest you think that the academic and scientific communities look upon mind control as a "tin foil hat" conspiracy, that is not the case. In fact, cult members have often spoken at the annual convention of the American Psychological Association, calling for informed discourse on the need for more understanding of mind control victims, especially those involved in destructive cults and religious movements (including terrorist groups). In "Mind Control: Psychological Reality of Mindless Rhetoric," for the November 2002 APA's President's Column, Dr. Philip G. Zimbardo writes: "A body of social science evidence shows that when systematically practiced by state-sanctioned police, military or destructive cults, mind control can induce false confessions, create converts who willingly torture or kill 'invented enemies,' engage indoctrinated members to work tireless, give up their money—and even their lives—for 'the cause.'" Zimbardo also goes on to say: "Understanding the dynamics and pervasiveness of situational power is essential to learning how to resist it and to weaken the dominance of the many agents of mind control who ply their trade daily on all of us behind many faces and fronts."

Those many faces and fronts include trusted authority figures, people in power, famous celebrities and world leaders, religious and spiritual figureheads and gurus, corporate giants, advertising agencies, the media, politicians, and even our own family and friends. We are assaulted on all fronts by people eager to take a piece of our minds and make them their own, for whatever purposes suit their agenda.

Pop Culture Mind Control

Our popular culture is filled with stories and images of what we think goes on when someone is brainwashed or under the influence of mind control tactics, whether by some mysterious government agency or a Svengali-like master manipulator on a more personal scale. War movies depict POWs being tortured and abused by their captors, even starved and deprived of sunlight and water, for the purposes of switching allegiances or coughing up valuable information. As a form of interrogation, manipulation of the mind and exposure of the body to extremes, such as heat, cold, deprivation, and beatings, can bring out the truth in even the most resisting person.

The term *brainwashing* actually comes to us from the Chinese, who used the phrase during the Maoist regime to describe the coercive techniques being used on individuals to get them into "right thinking" with the new social order. Brainwashing was first used in the English language in an article for the *Miami News* in October 1950 titled "Brain Washing Tactics Force Chinese Into Ranks of Communist Party," by reporter Edward Hunter. Hunter was actually a propaganda operative for the CIA working undercover as a journalist. Once the headline hit, the term stuck throughout the Cold War era and still is used to describe mind control techniques that literally "wash" the brain of thoughts, beliefs, and ideals, leaving it a clean slate for whatever those in control seek to write on it.

There has been a lot of controversy over whether or not POWs during the Korean War were victims of brainwashing tactics, which included prolonged interrogations designed to exhaust the victims, torture, and other abuses. The Army's own 1956 documents included in "Communist Interrogation, Indoctrination, and Exploitation of Prisoners of War" state that there is no verifiable proof of brainwashing and mind control as the reasons behind any POW abuse. Abuse did take place, no doubt, but was it for purposes of changing the minds of the captors? That has not been proven, although many people continue to propose that American GI POWs who defected to the enemy camp of the Chinese were brainwashed into doing so.

Even the CIA has been accused of creating the whole concept of brainwashing, as a means to explain why some POWs cut and ran, and sided *willingly* with the enemy camp. Yet there are those who believe the CIA was, and still is, actively involved in mind control experimentation of its own (as we dig into in a future chapter).

Licensed counselor and former member of the Unification Church Steven Alan Hassan, who now runs the Freedom of Mind Center, states on his Website that the most destructive forms of mind control are those that take the "locus of control" away from the individual, and that four basic tactics are used to manipulate and even change another person's individual identity: behavior, information, thoughts, and emotions. Tactics involving these four aspects prove to be the most successful in achieving control over another's entire mental reality and experience. This is most obvious in religious cults (which we explore in a later chapter), where isolation and the manipulation of information exposure can literally create an altered reality for the cult members—and not necessarily one they would choose voluntarily.

Our vision of mind control, brainwashing, and the possible reasons behind it often come from movies and spy novels, as well as headlines that scream of deadly cults and extreme religious indoctrination (you can join, but you can never unjoin!), satanic ritual abuse of children to create slaves with no independent will, the creation of the ultimate super soldier or warrior/spy, and the horrific human experimentation on unwilling victims in prisons or death camps using LSD or electroshock therapy. Rarely does anyone look deeper into the fiction and the media headlines to find the seeds of truth, or just the facts, ma'am. But the continuing popularity of conspiracy-related pop culture is a testament to the desire to know if we are being manipulated, how, and by whom.

From the earliest portrayals of mind control manipulators as strange, mad scientists performing hypnosis on poor, equally mad victims, to the more sophisticated stories today that combine fact and fiction and often feature actual technology being utilized by the manipulators (patented, too!), we love a good mind control story. Only when we stop, step back, and ask, "How much of this is story and how much might be real?" do we begin to grasp the serious nature of the subject and the depth of the rabbit hole it might take us down.

Probably the most well-known mind control–themed movie is *The Manchurian Candidate*, which began as a political thriller novel by Richard Condon and was adapted for the big screen twice: in 1962 featuring Frank Sinatra and Angela Lansbury in key roles, and in 2004 with Denzel Washington and Meryl Streep in the same roles. The story focuses on the son of a very prominent political family who is brainwashed into becoming a secret assassin. Set during the Korean War, Major Bennett Marco (played by Sinatra and later Washington) is kidnapped along with his platoon and taken to a place called Manchuria, where he and his unit are brainwashed. Later, upon returning to the States, Marco has horrible nightmares of betrayal and murder, at the hands of his sergeant, a man he thought was a hero. To avoid too many spoilers, basically Marco discovers others in his platoon suffering from said same nightmares, and uncovers a huge conspiracy involving brainwashing, sleeper assassins, and the potential assassination of a key political figure.

Behind it all is a powerful and quite evil bitch of a woman (played by Lansbury and later Streep), pulling the strings and the triggers behind the scenes.

The movie achieved critical acclaim for its acting, but also touched a nerve with audiences who had read about and heard of actual sleeper assassins and government-backed programs to create super soldiers (i.e., MKUltra; we will discuss that further later).

Another movie, *Conspiracy Theory*, introduces the MKUltra phenomenon to mainstream audiences courtesy of a crazy cab driver named Jerry, played by Mel Gibson, who tries to convince Alice, a lovely lawyer at the U.S. Justice Department, played by Julia Roberts, that his conspiracy blabberings are real, to tragic results. Sometimes, the crazy babble of a cab driver can actually be hiding the shattered memories and broken identity of a true MKUltra survivor—one who is starting to remember more and more. When he starts identifying men who are following him as CIA, Alice begins to pay attention, embroiling herself into the rabbit hole of conspiracy, which plays out with deadly results. This movie is chock full of classic MKUltra dialogue, torture, drugging, beating, stalking, harassment, terminology, and even triggers, which in this case is a copy of *Catcher in the Rye*. Triggers serve to "activate" sleeper assassins or agents into action, just as a trigger like clapping your hands might activate someone into (or out of) a hypnotic state.

Story Device

Using mind control as a device for story-telling purposes is not only popular, but deeply affecting, because these pop culture offerings suggest that we are all potential victims, and that, if "they" choose to control us, there is often nothing we can do but sit back and be controlled. Other films of note that come to mind include the spooky and mind-twisting *Shutter Island*, a 2010 psychological thriller, directed by the great Martin Scorsese, in which star Leonardo DiCaprio struggles with his own sanity, and identity, while investigating a strange disappearance at a remote asylum devoted to brain and mind manipulation studies. Another DiCaprio movie, *Inception*, suggested that we can even master the means of getting inside people's dreams and stealing their ideas.

Just a short sampling of some mind control/sleeper assassin /thought programming–themed entertainment would no doubt include:

- *Trilby* by George du Maurier
- *The Puppet Masters* by Robert A. Heinlein
- *Brave New World* by Aldous Huxley
- *1984* by George Orwell
- *Firestarter* by Stephen King
- *The Bourne Identity* book series by Robert Ludlum (also motion pictures)
- *A Clockwork Orange* by Anthony Burgess, later adapted into the classic Stanley Kubrick mindbender
- *The Terminal Man* by Michael Crichton
- *The Girl With the Dragon Tattoo* by Stieg Larsson

- *Telefon*, starring Charles Bronson
- *Gaslight*
- *The Matrix*
- *Scanners*
- *Dreamscape*
- *The Guyana Tragedy*
- *Jacob's Ladder*
- *Salt*, starring Angelina Jolie
- *The Long Kiss Goodnight*
- *The Sleep Room*
- *Hannah*
- *Femme Fatale*
- *Kill Bill*
- *Closet Land*
- *The Men Who Stare at Goats*, starring George Clooney
- *Total Recall*, starring Arnold Schwarzenegger
- *The X-Men* comic book series
- *The Prisoner* TV series
- *Falling Skies* TV series
- *Dark Skies* TV series
- *The X-Files* TV series
- *La Femme Nikita* TV series
- *The Pretender* TV series
- *Nowhere Man* TV series
- *Fringe* TV series
- *Homeland* TV series
- *Dollhouse* TV series
- *Legends* TV series
- *Blacklist* TV series

Even *Star Wars* gets in on the mind control action, with Jedi mind tricks allowing safe passage in dangerous places and control over both droids and humans. And good old Dr. Who wasn't above using the story device, either, with The Master controlling minds by a form of hypnosis. *Star Trek* offered us the alien Borgs creating a hive mind of subservients. It appears that, once again, our entertainment industry mirrors reality, because many of these shows, books, and stories feature elements that are actually true, buried amid the more imaginative—leaving we, the audience, to wonder and grow ever more paranoid over whether what we are seeing could really happen, or *did* happen, or is just the made-up stuff of the writers' minds. In the television series *Fringe*, lead scientist Walter Bishop sums it up in one episode, saying, "The brain is a computer, it's an organic computer. It can be hijacked like any other."

The previous list doesn't even *begin* to cover the use of mind control as a device in modern young adult (YA) dsytopic literature, and in various movies and television shows. Whether it is used as a means for controlling lesser classes of the population, or as a type of hypnosis to get someone to have sex with you, or as a means by which someone can make another person crazy—or even a killer—the theme is rampant and indicative of its importance to our struggles with individualism in a world that seems hell bent on keeping us all in one safe and submissive state. It is a struggle that speaks to our deepest psyche, where we exist in our most raw state, even as we fight for freedom of expression among our peers and our enemies.

Basically, it scares the shit out of us. Even as it empowers us. Knowledge is power, so they say.

And therein may lay the fascination with mind control–themed entertainment. We are uber protective of our bodies and our material goods, yet only when confronted with these stories, often ripped from actual headlines or conspiracy Websites, or declassified government documents, do we realize we may have forgotten to protect our minds.

Though we can somewhat understand the desire for finding workable mind programming techniques during wartime on behalf of authority figures eager to win at all costs, it becomes a bit harder to swallow why mind control might continue to be a goal in times of general comfort and calm. Certainly, we hear the conspiracy theories about a new world order or one mind/one religion, and about government and corporate entities that want to control the masses and even decide for them how they will vote, purchase, and consume. Yes, we hear the theories about how dumbing us down makes us a more compliant public. Yes, we know that there are people who want nothing more than to use the populace as puppets to help generate more wealth and power for the very few, who already have so much of it. But when it comes to really examining the reasons why mind control might be just as pervasive today as it always was, maybe even more so, the answer is always the same: People want to control other people.

Mind Control Motives

In a fascinating article for the Spring/Summer 2003 issue of *MKZine*, Dr. Allen Barker, a mind control expert and author with a powerhouse educational background, wrote about the "Motives for Mind Control." His suggestions still stand today, although with the rise of technology and surveillance, we can certainly add to the list. Some of his ideas include:

- Low-intensity warfare against the domestic population: using surveillance and harassment as a means to target anyone from a potential world leader to a whistleblower to activist groups.
- Stealing and mining ideas from others: spying and getting "inside the minds" of brilliant geniuses in other countries for their technology using covert methods of surveillance.
- Interrogation for secrets: an obvious method for wartime and terrorism, but could also be used on domestic soil to find out what your competition is up to.
- PSYOPS: psychological operations used in government and military programs.
- Suppression of technology: harassment, surveillance, and any method by which competition can be disabled.
- Hired harassment squads for billionaires: the rich and powerful can use mind control and surveillance/harassment methods to destroy competition and render their enemies useless, without hiring an actual hit man!
- To control a person, such as a world leader, a trained assassin, etc.: This would allow for a person groomed for a position of

power to take control with a massive support system behind him or her, albeit a covertly operating one. Also, super soldiers and assassins under mind control to take out important world figures.

○ To infiltrate a group: such as installing a puppet leader in a cult or religious sect to get information and inside knowledge.

○ Human guinea pigs for medical and psychological research.

○ To predict and preempt actions: like the movie *Minority Report*, there are those who not only want to *control* the behavior of others, but actually *predict* it, which becomes a more powerful method of control.

These are just a few of the motives behind mind control and harassment programs, whether done on a large scale by some government entity, or via a small religious cult or sect. The acknowledgment of MKUltra and the government's role in mind control programming proves this is happening, and that maybe what we have been exposed to is the tip of a gigantic iceberg, or one tentacle to a massive octopus whose reach permeates every aspect of our lives as individuals and as a collective.

Closer to Home

We cannot examine motives for the use of mind control on a large scale without also looking at how we as mere human mortals use our own techniques on a daily basis with the people in our circle of influence. The interesting thing about this subject matter is that when you bring it up, people automatically think of insidious, evil, sinister government torture and mind programming, or a powerful and insane cult leader calling his followers to kill themselves. Rarely do they think about the myriad ways they are trying to control, change, intimidate, suppress, or manipulate those around them—and vice versa. We engage in this behavior regularly, whether we want to admit it or not, *because it gets us a desired result*.

Ask yourself this: Do you know of someone who is the victim of domestic abuse, or child abuse? Do you know someone who is suffering at the hands of someone with narcissistic personality disorder? Do you know a sociopath, or psychopath, and have actually had to attempt to deal with one? There are a number of mental illnesses or, as some might label them, behavioral disorders that are perfect examples of people exercising control, often via emotional and/or physical harassment, manipulation, deception, abuse, and torture, over another person, or a child.

Let's take NPD, or narcissistic personality disorder, which seems to be rampant in today's "me and only me" culture. Not just famous actors and rock stars and athletes and politicians wear this label, but regular folks just like mothers and fathers, daughters and sons, lovers and colleagues. Even friends. The hallmarks of NPD are simple, and yet insidious, especially for those who have struggled with "narcs" in their own immediate environments.

In order for a person to be diagnosed with narcissistic personality disorder (NPD) he or she must meet five or more of the following symptoms (according to the American Psychiatric Association's "The Diagnostic and Statistical Manual of Mental Disorders"):

- Has a grandiose sense of self-importance (e.g., exaggerates achievements and talents, expects to be recognized as superior without commensurate achievements).
- Is preoccupied with fantasies of unlimited success, power, brilliance, beauty, or ideal love.
- Believes that he or she is "special" and unique, and can only be understood by, or should associate with, other special or high-status people (or institutions).
- Requires excessive admiration.
- Has a very strong sense of entitlement (e.g., unreasonable expectations of especially favorable treatment or automatic compliance with his or her expectations).
- Is exploitative of others (e.g., takes advantage of others to achieve his or her own ends).
- Lacks empathy (e.g., is unwilling to recognize or identify with the feelings and needs of others).
- Is often envious of others or believes that others are envious of him or her.
- Regularly shows arrogant, haughty behaviors or attitudes.

Now, although that may account for about 80 percent of the people you know, true narcissism becomes a powerful form of mind control over a victim in that these predatory individuals, similar to sociopaths and psychopaths, use a variety of deceptive and manipulative behaviors to totally undermine their victims and destroy their very identity. These behaviors include:

- Love bombing their victims and putting them on a pedestal in the first phases of the relationship, only to devalue and discard victims later.
- Lying, cheating, and deceiving with a strong sense of entitlement because the narcissist believes he deserves to use whatever means necessary to get what he wants.
- Projection and mirroring of her own sins, faults, and weaknesses onto the victim.
- Gas lighting—the process of undermining the sanity of the victim by lying, changing stories, contradicting oneself, denying, and even using the silent treatment to punish the victim.
- Narcissistic rage, or breaking out into unreasonably violent or virulent anger fits or rages when caught in a lie, cheating, deceiving, or when called out on bad behaviors.
- Isolating the victim to make it easier to control him or her.
- Stalking, harassing, and even threatening the victim to create an environment of fear and paranoia.
- Physical, sexual, and emotional abuse, and even murder.

Not all narcissists reach some of these extremes, as there are "functioning" narcissists who can actually be quite successful members of society, even as there are "malignant narcissists" who are far more damaged and damaging, but the means by which they use mind programming, undermining, control, and brainwashing techniques to keep their victims co-dependent and emotionally fragile mirror many of the same methods used to dismantle the identities of men and women during cult indoctrinations, POW interrogations, and trauma abuse rituals (more on that later). Sociopaths and psychopaths take these behaviors to an even higher extreme than the average narcissist, and have become so much a part of our modern culture, we tend to revere and celebrate these people, even as they commit behaviors that would not be acceptable otherwise.

Abuse and Control

The links between narcissism and mind control are many. The need for utter and complete control over another is one of the diagnostic tools used by psychologists to define narcissistic personality disorder. People suffering from narcissism attempt to control others in order to enhance their own sense of power and entitlement. Narcissists must preserve their self-image at all costs, often while they devalue others to increase their own sense of self-worth. Narcissists have a strong sense of entitlement and believe they deserve special recognition for their intelligence and skills. Unfortunately, they also believe that because of their superiority, they have the God-given right to exploit, demean, and use others. And because their victims usually start out feeling as though the narcissist loved them, the recovery from this kind of emotional vampirism is difficult. An anonymous post on a narcissism forum sums up this most pervasive kind of mind control: *"There is nothing worse than being set upon maliciously by someone you believed you could trust, someone you love, and someone you thought loved you and had your best interests at heart."*

These are the same behaviors exacted upon the public by tyrants and dictators, who will overlook and excuse torture, abuse, and even widespread slaughter because of their own self-righteousness. A tight rein of control over the hearts and minds of others in a necessity in any domineering relationship, whether between an abusive husband and his long-suffering wife, or an evil political or religious leader who believes he or she is the chosen one, superior to others.

Domestic abuse is not all that different from dictatorship abuse. In fact, some of the worst psychopaths the world has ever known have been determined by psychologists to often exhibit quite normal personality characteristics, including those responsible for war crimes. *The New Yorker* political theorist Hannah Arendt called this "banality of evil." Arendt covered the 1961 war crimes trial of Adolf Eichmann, who was examined before his trial by several psychiatrists. They unanimously declared Eichmann "normal." Arendt later wrote in her book *Eichmann in Jerusalem: A Report on the Banality of Evil*: "The trouble with Eichmann was precisely that so many were like him, and that the many were neither perverted nor sadistic, that they were, and still are, terribly and terrifyingly normal. From the viewpoint of our legal institutions and of our moral standards of judgment, this normality was much more terrifying than all the atrocities put together."

The idea that mind control abusers can be considered in any way "normal," including those who commit the most heinous atrocities against humanity, is disturbing. But it's true. We use narcissism as an example of how mind control doesn't always have to look the way our entertainment industry portrays it, like Frank Sinatra being brainwashed in *The Manchurian Candidate* or some sexy female sleeper assassin being given a verbal trigger to kill a Congressman. Sometimes, the battle for the mind occurs on a much closer and much more normal, intimate level.

Sometimes it even occurs at home.

2

RITUALS AND RITES: MIND CONTROL IN OUR PAST

Rituals, anthropologists will tell us, are about transformation. The rituals we use for marriage, baptism or inaugurating a president are as elaborate as they are because we associate the ritual with a major life passage, the crossing of a critical threshold, or in other words, with transformation.
—Abraham Verghese

It is clear that rituals and sacrifices can bring people together, and it may well be that a group that does such things has an advantage over one that does not. But it is not clear why a religion has to be involved. Why are gods, souls, an afterlife, miracles, divine creation of the universe, and so on brought in?
—Paul Bloom

Even in ancient cultures, ritual practices were used to control and change the mindset, and the thought processes, behaviors, and beliefs, of others. Often this was done to mirror what it was believed the deities wanted—the Gods and Goddesses that demanded loyalty and total submission. Yet there were also plenty of human authority figures that demanded the same.

Our ancient ancestors used ritual to not just worship, but to set about certain rules and agreements initiates would follow. Those rules sometimes were set out for the populace as well, in the form of religious doctrine and dogma, itself a type of cultish brainwashing we will discuss more in a later chapter. Ritual was a way of formalizing belief, understanding, knowledge, and even expectation. Ritual often created group identity as well as individual identity, thus the popularity of secret societies with carefully chosen membership.

Rituals

The word *ritual* comes from the Latin *ritualis*, which means "that which pertains to rite," or a particular or proven way of doing something, as in a custom. Ritual is a process or sequence of activities that involve gestures, spoken or read words, symbols, numbers, objects, and movements. We perform rituals all the time, from funerals and marriages to frat house "rushes" to swearing on the Holy Bible before a judge and jury. Rituals don't always have to be performed in a secretive location, but they do seem to be characterized by six factors: formalism, traditionalism, invariance, rule-governance, sacral symbolism, and performance, according to Catherine Bell, an American religious and ritual studies scholar, and author of *Ritual Theory, Ritual Practice* and *Ritual: Perspectives and Dimensions*.

Bell wrote that ritual utilized a limited and organized code of expressions that induced a formal style capable of rendering rebellion impossible. Formalism fixes the ritual and induces acceptance and compliance. Traditionalism appeals to the historical, such as a Thanksgiving or New Year's ritual, which may or may not be formal. Invariance evokes a physical discipline, as in careful choreography of ritual actions, and is often seen in group rituals. Rule-governance is a formalized ritual involving specific rules that impose an order on behavior of groups, often useful in wartime. Sacred symbolism appeals to the more religious, metaphysical, or supernatural bent using a particular object or symbol that evokes allegiance and loyalty, such as the American flag or a medal of honor. Performance adds a theatrical bent to ritual, such as singing and dancing, to help shape the experiences of those involved in the ritual, as well as those viewing it.

We use rituals that combine one or more of these characteristics for:

○ Rites of passage such as marriage, circumcision, debutante balls, fraternity, and sororities.

○ Calendrical rites that mark a specific date or time of year, such as eating black-eyed peas on New Year's Day, or going around the Thanksgiving table and expressing gratitude.

○ Communion and exchange rites with a religious connotation, such as offering foods to the deities or taking Communion at a Catholic church.

○ Festivals and fasting rites that celebrate on a community level a religious or spiritual tradition, or a carnival-style festival that brings community together.

○ Rites of affliction that are designed to mitigate angry spirits or gods or heal a community member, including exorcising someone thought to be possessed by demons!

One of the most interesting aspects of rituals and rites is their ability to create a form of social control, by regulating and stabilizing the social interactions of a group. Rituals keep order amid chaos and often give individuals a role to play that adds to the functionality of the group. As a form of structure, ritual modifies behavior to fit within the confines of the desired structure, and anyone who breaks the ritual or refuses to partake is considered a rebel or an enemy, playing upon the desire of human beings to belong to a community and be "one of the gang."

Taken to an extreme, ritual can be used to also discipline or punish, as utilized by monks during medieval times, when monastic orders demanded strict disciplines be followed. Those monks who broke the rules paid the price with prayer and fasting that could become quite taxing on the body and spirit. Rituals would be performed to make penance for their sins, sometimes over and over again, until it was determined by an authority figure that the monk had made amends internally and externally. The point was to teach monks emotional and physical control via the practice of repeated rituals.

To some, the use of ritual leads to a sense of collective identity, or belonging to a group, which of course made it much easier to control the individual. But is it really mind control?

Obeying the Gods

Take, for example, ancient Egyptian religion, which looked for all intents and purposes like a cult created around the desire to interact with the deities through specific rituals. This may not look like a typical form of mind control, and certainly doesn't compare with government experimentation on innocent victims, but the use of ritual is definitely a form of behavior modification, as is religious doctrine, designed to get a certain group of people to think and behave a certain way.

In the case of the Egyptians, priests in the temples of worship enforced rituals to honor and obey the will of the Gods and Goddesses, and lower-class members of society were expected to go along with those rituals and ceremonies. Offerings and anointing to appease the deities and win favor were among the rituals, as was the spread of knowledge and wisdom.

This cultish ritual-focused activity was present in all the great cultures of the past, including the Roman, Greek, and Mesoamerican. A hierarchy of priests and even priestesses was established to create order and to separate levels of honor, wisdom, and occult knowledge from lower classes that might not appreciate the information. Not only that, but the deities themselves were organized into hierarchies, with primary and secondary cults honoring various Gods and Goddesses based upon importance and necessity. Deities considered lower men and women on the totem pole got less followers and less press, and held power mostly on a more local scale. The big dogs took the honors as the cults of choice, and more people took part in those rituals on a more regional scale.

This same behavior is evident in the cults of today, where cult leaders create a hierarchy among their followers to keep order. We even see this in our military, government, and judicial systems, which often act as though embedded in rituals themselves, in the form of governance and authority.

These ancient cults were often called "mystery cults," and devotees often displayed a number of behaviors we today might consider barbaric and even violent, but all in honor of the chosen deity. Sacrifices of humans and animals, ritual torture, and sex rituals were commonplace, though perhaps not practiced in the direct light of day. The darker sides of both deities and humans were expressed via these occult and rather graphic practices, often highly symbolic of the cycle of birth, life, death, and rebirth. Initiates were expected to do what they were told, and what the Gods and Goddesses told them. Individuality was forsaken for the cause of groupthink. The many pre-Christian cults that existed during the Roman Empire, for example, used pagan rituals and beliefs in the form of festivals, celebrations, and rites that honored the deities of the natural world, including those deities that represented the darker elements of human existence. Think sex, orgies, Saturnalia, and other commemorations that were intended to honor the powers and forces behind creation, life, and destruction.

The Cult of Dionysus in ancient Greece has a reputation for the more decadent and even downright creepy practices. Take their predilection for ritual hangings. Honoring the Olympic God included more mundane things like offering sacrifices of fruits and rams, and even drinking vast quantities of wine, as Dionysus was the God of fertility and wine. Sex was a part of the rituals, to honor, of course, reproduction and fertility. But those who chose to celebrate the Anthesteria Festival of Athens went even further. On the third day of the festival, women called Aletides, after Aletis, a mythological figure who hung herself in the legend of Icarius, hang themselves from ropes tied to wooden beams to symbolize the suffering and death of poor Aletis. No, the women don't hang themselves to *death*, thankfully. (The hanging is a symbolic act and women do not actually die!) But their devotion to their deities shows a willingness to behave in certain ways that mirror today's cults. Yet today, cult members often actually kill themselves.

The Phrygian Goddess Kybele represented both fertility and nature. She was also the mother of Dionysus in ancient Greece, and considered the great Mother of the Gods. To honor her in festival meant engaging in orgiastic dancing and drinking, song, and even traditional self-mutilation. The excitement of the festival would build to such a frenzied extreme that devotees would begin beating themselves with leather thongs. Priests of this nature cult would even castrate themselves and anoint the festival decorations with their own blood. One must imagine the type of frenzied celebration that would lead to such self-inflicted violence, but in a religious context, or the context of "worship," it seems that people lose control of their minds quite easily.

Not to ignore the East, let's look at the Aghori or Aghouri, a Hindu cult with ancient roots that worships Shiva (one of the primary forms of God in the Hindu Smarta tradition, the destroyer and transformer) with great fervor and are thought to have splintered from the 14th-century Kapaika order. The Aghori followers utilize some pretty disgusting rituals to honor the Brahman, which is the all that includes even evil and death, including eating the rotting flesh of animals, and even animal feces, to become enlightened. They end their rituals by consuming the flesh of a dead and decaying human. That a ritual includes cannibalism speaks volumes to the power of religious belief to make people do some really crazy, even grotesque things, under the mental control of the powers and forces they wish to favor or honor.

Again, we will discuss modern cults later, but the idea here is that our ancestors allowed the modification of their beliefs and behaviors in accordance with the perceived desires of the deities they adored, or feared. This is not much different from those who are brainwashed by the media, religious and political groups, and even their own governments in an attempt to create a specific result in behavior in an individual, a group, or even an entire nation.

Secret Societies

Secret societies throughout our history, such as the Templars, the KKK, the Freemasons, and other groups that operate under the radar and with elaborately structured ritualistic methods, often incorporate the same types of behavior modification methods when dealing with keeping initiates and members on track and in line. That is part and parcel of being a part of a secret society, even something as silly sounding as a college fraternity, where initiates are expected to do some pretty rotten things to prove their worth—even things that go against their morals, values, and belief systems. All in the name of belonging, initiates might even be called upon to alter their entire perceptions of the world around them and ascribe to a particular world view, including one that espouses racism, sexism, abuse, violence, aggression, and humiliation—to self and others.

Whether using drugs and potions concocted to alter consciousness, some type of sensory deprivation, physical and emotional stress, or psychological manipulations, initiates and members were symbolically being cleansed and purified for their service into the organization, just as a baby might be baptized in a tub of holy water to become a Christian. Again, harking back to the priestly initiates of the ancient Roman, Greek, and Egyptian cults, secret rituals were designed to transform the person to another level of conscious awareness to commune or bond symbolically with the chosen deity. This could be best achieved by either depriving the initiate of sensory experience, or overwhelming him with it. In both cases, the desired mental state was achieved.

Secret societies are often associated with Satanism and devil worship, and that association has given rise to all kinds of allegations of horrific abuse, child sacrifice and sexual abuse, animal slaughter, and even adult sacrifice, all in the name of serving some deity—but also as a means of controlling members with fear and the terror of punishment. In order to belong to a secret society in the first place, one must swear allegiances to the order, even if those allegiances go against the person's own integrity, personal values, and family duties. Talk about mind control. These darker allegations have been leveled at the Freemasons most of all, perhaps because they possess the most enigmatic of profiles. Their humble origin as a society of masons who took great pride in their work has now morphed into a powerful Illuminati-like figurehead that uses rituals and symbols to promote a hidden agenda on the entire world.

In many ways, secret societies are cults that operate on a much more implicate, hidden level—much less public about their goals, agendas, and membership rosters than the majority of cults (who often seek out publicity to gain new converts).

Rituals were important during the Middle Ages, to keep the populace in line with the strict and often-oppressive religious and political beliefs and agendas. But ritual wasn't the only way to keep someone from doing his or her own thing. Mental illness has always been around, as long as humanity has, and for those who may have been schizophrenic or suffering from some form of PTSD or personality disorder, it was often assumed they were under the possession of demons or evil deities. An early practice was to cut a hole in the skull of the person believed to be possessed, called trephining, in order to free the demon and allow it escape. Sometimes an instrument would be inserted into the brain to help the demon out, which can be described as an early lobotomy. If the person deemed possessed suffered from permanent brain damage, oh well. At least their erratic behavior was now under complete control.

The Use of Torture

Exorcisms during the Middle Ages were performed on women who didn't quite obey the rules and traditions of the day. These were always performed by a group of men, of course, and followed the "witch-hunting Bible" known as the *Malleus Maleficarum*, written in 1484, which included strict forms of interrogation and torture methods designed to

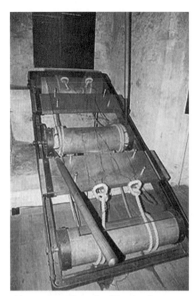

A torture rack in the Tower of London, England. Image © David Bjorgen. Made available via Wikimedia Commons.

get a confession. This was the tool of the Inquisitions and throughout the Middle Ages, it was utilized as a means for excusing the slaughter of innocent women, children, and men who would end up confessing to sins they were not guilty of.

Early torture devices included restraint chairs, wooden cribs and restraint beds, shock treatments, isolation, and sensory deprivation that drove out not just demons, but false confessions, even as they drove many a poor victim insane. Shock treatments might involve the use of electrical jolts, being blindfolded and dunked in vats of water, being bombarded with extremely loud noises, or being put in a rotating chair that brought about nausea and even loss of consciousness. Violence and torture were seen as perfectly natural and acceptable ways of ridding women of their inner demons, even if their only sin was making a healing brew out of natural herbs. But violence was often not even necessary, for many an innocent coughed up a false confession just under duress of constant and forceful interrogation methods that would make the Nazis proud, and in fact, were the foundation for torture- and trauma-based interrogations of future dictators and despots, religious and political.

The methods and mechanisms of torture during the Middle Ages were brutal at best, horrific at their worst. Many were designed to actually kill the victim, or come very close. Some were no doubt more about the pleasure they gave the torturer, who must have felt such power controlling another human being. Some of the favorite devices of medieval times include:

The coffin torture: Placing the victim in a coffin for hours or even days without food or water.

The rack: The victim is strapped to a table and her limbs are stretched to the point of near dismemberment.

The Spanish tickler: Used to tear the victim's flesh apart during the Spanish Inquisition.

Water torture: A primitive form of the waterboarding used today, where the victim is dunked under restraint into a lake or pond or tub of water.

The garrotte: A hanging device used mostly in Spain for executions.

The heretic fork: A painful restraint used during the Middle Ages and the Spanish Inquisition.

The wheel: The victim was restrained to a large wooden wheel that would spin for hours, sometimes days, often causing death.

Fire torture: Favored during the witch trials and burnings, where mainly women and children were tied to wooden stakes and burned upon woodpiles.

The Judas cradle: The victim was tied to a triangular-shaped seat and slowly impaled to death.

These are but a very few of the imaginative means by which religious and political figures during the darkest of times destroyed the minds, bodies, and spirits of those they deemed dangerous or heretic. The idea was to force a confession, control the behav-

17th-century woodcut of a woman being dunked into the river in a cucking chair. Image made available by Wikimedia Commons.

ior, or outright kill the person, whichever suited the dirty deed the victim was thought to be guilty of. Today we continue to use modified versions of these devices in psych wards and institutions, under the guise of controlling behavior and restraining violent psychopaths. But one has to wonder: Who is the real psychopath—the person being tortured, or the torturer?

Though crude and barbaric, and totally lacking in finesse, these forms of mind control and behavior modification worked, sometimes so well that the victim died, thus eliciting the control on behalf of those doling out the torture. What better way to scare a society than to torture and kill those who color outside the lines and sing out of harmony? What better way to control someone than with fear—fear of pain, of suffering, of watching the suffering of others, and of death? These are powerful tools for altering behavior, even changing his or her mind completely.

In the next chapter we will see how fear moved from the domain of controlling personal behavior to the larger domain of war. The victims are no longer women and children believed to be possessed by demons or in cahoots with the devil as witches, but instead men, women, and children groomed to be assassins, super soldiers, and spies.

3

Of Monarchs, Bluebirds, and Artichokes: MKUltra and Mind Control in Modern Times

Perhaps the best spy is one who does not even know he or she is a spy...
—Dr. Allen Barker, "Motives for Mind Control"

Only the small secrets need to be protected. The big ones are kept secret by public incredulity.
—Marshall McLuhan

Today, we have stores where you can take a basic teddy bear body, and add onto it all kinds of accoutrements and accessories. It's called "Build-A-Bear," and there are dozens of franchises across the nation. Any child can design his or her own "perfect" bear buddy according to particular likes and preferences. You pay for the materials you use and walk out with the bear of your dreams.

There are those within our government, military, and corporate complex (and most of us know by now the three work closely together) that have tried to do the very same thing with people: building the perfect spy. Building the perfect assassin. Building the perfect weapon.

The MKUltra Era

Mind control has been the modus operandi of choice. From the early 1950s into the early 1970s, the CIA was involved in mind control research under the name of Project MKUltra. Thanks to a number of declassified documents obtained through the Freedom of Information Act

(FOIA), we now know that, along with the Special Operations Division of the Army's Chemical Corps, a specialized sector of the CIA, known as the Scientific Intelligence Division, performed a variety of experiments with the assistance of dozens of colleges, prisons, institutions, and hospitals, many of them illegal and without victims' approval or willingness, involving mind control, behavior modification, LSD and chemical exposure, sensory deprivation, and even sexual abuse and torture.

Many of the victims were children.

MKUltra ushered in an era of invasive and abusive experimentation on human subjects under the guise of government and/or military entities and institutions, that had in its origins and roots the torture and brainwashing methods taught to U.S. government agents by former Nazi scientists, who were recruited into the United States after World War II as part of "Operation Paperclip." Along with MKUltra, projects included such monikers as Bluebird, Artichoke, Delta, Span, Chatter, and even Monarch—all cover names for mind control and behavior modification experiments that should never have happened.

But they did, both here in the United States and in Canada, and we have eyewitness testimony of many of those experimented upon, as well as documents now made public, to shine a light on a truly dark part of our modern historical record. That our own government was capable of performing chemical, biological, and even radiological forms of mind control experimentation on the unsuspecting public is chilling enough, but even more chilling when the goals were revealed: to create spies and counter-spies. Super soldiers and trained assassins. Manchurian candidates programmed to kill. All they had to do was destroy the will and mind and personality—and replace them with those that they, the "handlers," wanted.

Sleeper agents that, once activated, would do anything they were programmed and trained to do, carrying out dangerous missions without a second thought, and never remembering a thing afterwards. This, along with better and more effective interrogation methods, appears to be the main goal behind the intense interest and experimentation into the depths of the human mind. If you could use torture to extract information, you could certainly also use it to *put in* information—and tell the mind to forget it after the deed was done.

MKUltra and its associated projects were designed to see how far the human mind could be destroyed, altered, and rebuilt for purposes of covert operations—building a better spy and soldier, and breaking the enemy in new and creative ways. From giving victims LSD to the use of hypnosis to repeated sexual and physical abuse, the tactics and techniques once perfected in Nazi Germany in concentration camps could now be perfected to use both on and off the battleground for our own advantage.

The name MKUltra itself tells a story. An offshoot and progressive evolution of earlier Projects Chatter, Bluebird, and Artichoke, all involved in mind control and interrogation methods, MKUltra got its name from the use of the letters *MK* to signify any project sponsored by the CIA's Technical Services Staff. *Ultra* signified the most top-secret level of classified World War II intelligence programs. Allen Welsh Dulles, the CIA director during 1953, ordered MKUltra into existence as a means of developing mind control drugs to use against enemies, including the Soviets, once it was learned that our own POWs were being tested with drugs during the Korean War. Sidney Gottlieb was chosen to head up the project, which many researchers suggest was a direct result of "red dread" and Communist paranoia.

Unfortunately, most of the MKUltra records were destroyed at the command of CIA Director Richard Helms in 1973, but in 1977, an FOIA request revealed more than 20,000 documents that had skipped notice, and that led to the Church Committee investigations, led by Senator Frank Church, into the alleged mind control and drug experiments being undertaken by U.S. intelligence agencies. Senate hearings were held in 1977, after President Gerald Ford had issued an executive order banning experimentation with drugs on human subjects, unless they gave consent. The hearings, led by the Senate Select Committee on Intelligence, further examined the MKUltra documents and allegations and found enough evidence of the extensive testing on unwitting citizens, and one death as a result: that of Frank Olson, a U.S. Army biochemist and bio-warfare researcher who his family claims was given LSD without his consent as part of the CIA's drug experimentation program under chemist Sidney Gottlieb. He died a week later. His family believed he was murdered because of the highly classified information he was privy to,

DRAFT ▓▓▓▓ *A*
9 June 1953

MEMORANDUM FOR THE RECORD

SUBJECT: Project MKULTRA, Subproject 8

     1. Subproject 8 is being set up as a means to continue the present work in the general field of L.S.D. at ▓▓▓▓▓▓▓▓ *B* ▓▓▓▓▓ until 11 September 1954.

     2. This project will include a continuation of a study of the biochemical, neurophysiological, sociological, and clinical psychiatric aspects of L.S.D., and also a study of L.S.D. antagonists and drugs related to L.S.D., such as L.A.E. A detailed proposal is attached. *C* The principle investigators will continue to be ▓▓▓▓▓▓▓▓▓ *C B* ▓▓▓▓▓▓▓▓▓▓▓▓▓▓ all of ▓▓▓▓▓▓▓▓▓▓ *B*

     3. The estimated budget of the project at ▓▓▓▓▓▓▓ *B* is $39,500.00. The ▓▓▓▓▓▓▓▓▓▓ will serve as a *B* cut-out and cover for this project and will furnish the above funds to the ▓▓▓▓▓▓▓▓▓▓▓ as a philanthropic grant for *B* medical research. A service charge of $790.00 (2% of the estimated budget) is to be paid to the ▓▓▓▓▓▓▓▓ for this service. *B*

     4. Thus the total charges for this project will not exceed $40,290.00 for a period ending September 11, 1954.

     5. ▓▓▓▓▓▓▓▓▓▓▓▓ (Director of the *C* hospital) are cleared through TOP SECRET and are aware of the true purpose of the project.

[signature]

[signature] ▓▓▓▓▓▓▓▓ *A*
Chemical Division/TSS

APPROVED:

[signature]

Chief, Chemical Division/TSS

▓▓▓▓▓▓▓ PROGRAM ▓▓▓▓▓

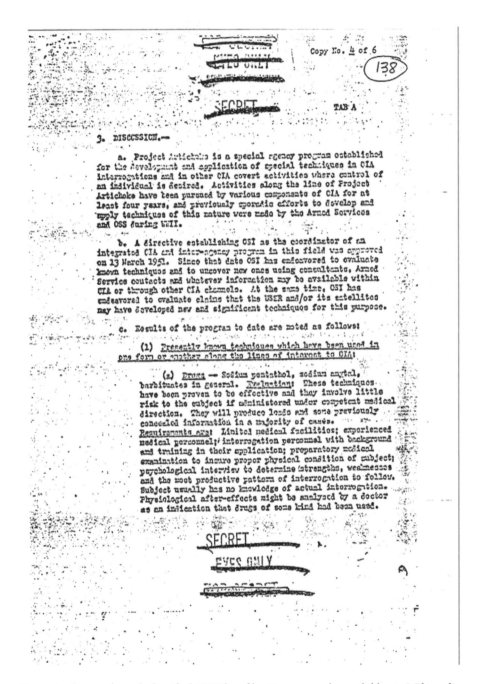

Copy No. 4 of 6

138

SECRET   TAB A

3. DISCUSSION.—

a. Project Artichoke is a special agency program established for the development and application of special techniques in CIA interrogations and in other CIA covert activities where control of an individual is desired. Activities along the line of Project Artichoke have been pursued by various components of CIA for at least four years, and previously sporadic efforts to develop and apply techniques of this nature were made by the Armed Services and OSS during WII.

b. A directive establishing OSI as the coordinator of an integrated CIA and inter-agency program in this field was approved on 13 March 1952. Since that date OSI has endeavored to evaluate known techniques and to uncover new ones using consultants, Armed Service contacts and whatever information may be available within CIA or through other CIA channels. At the same time, OSI has endeavored to evaluate claims that the USSR and/or its satellites may have developed new and significant techniques for this purpose.

c. Results of the program to date are noted as follows:

(1) Presently known techniques which have been used in one form or another along the lines of interest to CIA:

(a) Drugs — Sodium pentathol, sodium amytal, barbituates in general. Evaluation: These techniques have been proven to be effective and they involve little risk to the subject if administered under competent medical direction. They will produce leads and some previously concealed information in a majority of cases. Requirements are: Limited medical facilities; experienced medical personnel; interrogation personnel with background and training in their application; preparatory medical examination to insure proper physical condition of subject; psychological interview to determine strengths, weaknesses and the most productive pattern of interrogation to follow. Subject usually has no knowledge of actual interrogation. Physiological after-effects might be analyzed by a doctor as an indication that drugs of some kind had been used.

SECRET

EYES ONLY

Two actual pages from declassified MKUltra files. Images made available via Wikimedia Commons.

and that he had been marked as a security risk, especially because, just before his death, he had quit his high-level position as chief of the Special Operations Division, citing a moral crisis of conscience over his involvement in biological warfare and assassination training materials, as well as the involvement of Nazi scientists from Operation Paperclip. His death, falling from a 13-story window, was at first considered suicide, but the medical examiner's report in 1994, after his body was exhumed, determined the cause of death to be homicide.

It appeared that the CIA and others involved had no qualms about killing one of their own if he or she was possibly about to blow the whistle.

Canada held its own hearings in the form of a scathing news show, *The Fifth Estate*, that exposed to the public the Canadian government's involvement and financial contributions to the experiments. The Canadian government eventually settled citizen lawsuits out of court and awarded $100,000 to 127 victims, according to an article by Karin Goodwin in *The Sunday Times*.

Many conspiracy theorists posit that these experiments, which were said to have ended officially in the 1970s, no doubt after declassified docs and government hearings set the public and the media on fire, are still going on, albeit under the radar and with different names to hide their connections to the original MKUltra.

Dozens of books have been written detailing the rise of MKUltra, so we don't wish to reinvent the wheel, but what made this time period so important is the combination of "them" paranoia with the desire to control the enemy, certainly something alive and well even today with new paranoia aimed at terrorist groups and ongoing war in the Middle East. That our government would go to the lengths suggested by the released documents and witness testimony that it did to attempt to control and create human weapons is terrifying. What is even more terrifying is the fact that it was all done relatively in secret and the government managed to destroy most of the most damning evidence. Enough remains that we can all read about the abusive and insidious experimentation on men, women, and even children, designed to take away humanity and replace it with machine-like responses to built-in requests.

Scope of Studies

One of the Senate hearing documents, written in 1955, conveys some of the scope of the studies and experiments, many using mind-altering substances, under the MKUltra program:

- Substances that will promote illogical thinking and impulsiveness to the point where the recipient would be discredited in public.
- Substances [that] increase the efficiency of mentation and perception.
- Materials [that] will cause the victim to age faster/slower in maturity.
- Materials [that] will promote the intoxicating effect of alcohol.
- Materials [that] will produce the signs and symptoms of recognized diseases in a reversible way so that they may be used for malingering, etc.
- Materials that will cause temporary/permanent brain damage and loss of memory.
- Substances that will enhance the ability of individuals to withstand privation, torture, and coercion during interrogation and so-called "brain-washing."
- Materials and physical methods that will produce amnesia for events preceding and during their use.
- Physical methods of producing shock and confusion over extended periods of time and capable of surreptitious use.
- Substances that produce physical disablement such as paralysis of the legs, acute anemia, etc.
- Substances [that] will produce a chemical that can cause blisters.
- Substances [that] alter personality structure in such a way that the tendency of the recipient to become dependent upon another person is enhanced.
- A material [that] will cause mental confusion of such a type that the individual under its influence will find it difficult to maintain a fabrication under questioning.

- ○ Substances [that] will lower the ambition and general working efficiency of men when administered in undetectable amounts.

- ○ Substances [that] promote weakness or distortion of the eyesight or hearing faculties, preferably without permanent effects.

- ○ A knockout pill [that] can surreptitiously be administered in drinks, food, cigarettes, as an aerosol, etc., which will be safe to use, provide a maximum of amnesia, and be suitable for use by agent types on an ad hoc basis.

- ○ A material [that] can be surreptitiously administered by the above routes and which in very small amounts will make it impossible for a person to perform physical activity.

Source: "Senate MKUltra Hearing: Appendix C—Documents Referring to Subprojects," page 167 (in PDF document page numbering). Senate Select Committee on Intelligence a Committee on Human Resources. August 3, 1977.

Paperclips and Programming:
The Nazi Mind Control Connection

Few people realize that after we fought the Nazis in World War II, our own government, under the direction of the Joint Intelligence Objectives Agency (JIOA), actually brought some of their best scientists and researchers to the United States from Germany as part of a program called Project Paperclip, aka Operation Overcast. Scientists and their families were quietly relocated in the States, especially those specializing in rocketry, weapons, and aerodynamics, to learn their secrets before the Soviets could. Almost 1,800 of these Nazi scientists (and their family members) headed for places like White Sands Proving Ground, Fort Strong, and Fort Bliss, all under the radar of even State Department officials. They were geophysicists, opticians, engineers, chemists, physicists, intelligence officers, electronics experts, medical researchers, and aerodynamic engineers, and they included high-ranking Nazi figures such as Wernher von Braun, Wilhelm Jungert, Fritz Mueller, Reinhard Gehlen, and Theodor Popol.

Even the United States Bureau of Mines imported several German synthetic fuel scientists to a chemical plant in Missouri.

The goal was to utilize these Nazi scientists and extract their extensive knowledge as a way to get a leg up in the Cold War against the Soviets. These very same men who helped Adolf Hitler develop sarin gas and weaponized plague, some of whom later were to stand trial for war crimes, were given security clearances and helped the United States get the upper hand in a pending battle for world dominance. President Harry Truman didn't even know of the project, as the JIOA created false records of employment, and even false identities and biographies, for the new scientists, going so far as to literally destroy any records of former Nazi affiliation.

On July 19, 1945, the Joint Chiefs of Staff held a number of scientists from the German Army Rocket Center, of which Werner von Braun was the technical director, at a place called Camp Overcast. The orders were to keep tabs on the scientists until their intelligence and knowledge were tapped. Only then would releasing them be considered. The project was called Operation Overcast, until the location was leaked and the name was changed to Project Paperclip a year later.

Journalist Annie Jacobsen, in her definitive look at the Paperclip program, Operation Paperclip: The Secret Intelligence Program That Brought Nazi Scientists to America, asks the question: "Does accomplishment cancel out past crimes?" Her book documents the roles the Nazi scientists played, even in coming up with new means of using LSD in mind control and interrogation experiments done at a secret site in Germany, and shows how these men were later treated like heroes and given great admiration and acclaim for the knowledge they gave our government officials. Jacobsen writes, "Some officials believed that by endorsing the Paperclip program, they were accepting the lesser of two evils—that if American didn't recruit these scientists, the Soviet Communists surely would. Other generals and colonels admired and respected these men and said so."

Talk about strange bedfellows.

Cameron and Key Figures

One of the key figures in the MKUltra program, other than Sidney Gottlieb, was a man named Donald Ewen Cameron. The Scottish psychiatrist became involved with the Canadian side of the MKUltra program after he was invited in 1943 to McGill University in Montreal, where the Allen Memorial Institute of Psychiatry was founded with generous grants from the Rockefeller Foundation, among others. Cameron already had a great reputation for his work in biologically linked psychiatry, and had become intrigued with the idea of manipulating the brain and controlling memory. Now he was the head honcho at a major university and had the ability to begin experimenting with what he called "psychic driving," which basically involved putting subjects into a drug-induced or insulin-induced coma for periods of time during which they were forced to listen to a looped tape that Cameron and his technicians had created. The tapes consisted of positive messages that were supposed to wipe clean the existing mental programming of the subject and implant memories on a clean slate.

Cameron's intentions may have been good, but his techniques, which also involved massive electro-shock treatments and LSD experimentation, often administered without the consent of the subjects, were later described as torture by patients and even critics. It was these experiments, especially the psychic driving, that got the attention of a U.S. army colonel, and soon Cameron was being briefed on brainwashing techniques. The CIA began funding Cameron's experiments as part of MKUltra, and because these experiments were illegal on American soil, the money was secretly funneled into the Allen Memorial Institute of Psychiatry via New York's Cornell Institute, as later declassified docs would reveal. Several books exposed his darker side, including Anne Collins's 1989 book, *In the Sleep Room: The Story of CIA Brainwashing Experiments in Canada*, which documented the horrors that Cameron imposed upon people, many of whom suffered from milder disorders like anxiety and post-partum depression. According to Collins, by the time they got out of the infamous studies, they were left without decades of memories, even forgetting how to control their own bladders. Some did not even remember their own children. All of them were tortured by one man's attempts to "de-pattern" behaviors and memories, and replace them with Cameron's own programming.

In a 2007 edition of *The Scotsman*, Cameron's career was featured in an article titled "Stunning Tale of Brainwashing, the CIA and an Unsuspecting Scots Researcher." The article brings up a few good points: that Cameron didn't know his research was being funded by the American CIA (although that doesn't excuse the brutality of his methods by any means), and that some of his methods, like using massive doses of electroshock therapy, had worked to some success for alcoholics. But the article looks at the uglier side of a man obsessed with his own methods, interviewing one of the hundreds of victims or subjects that were experimented upon in Cameron's own "sleep room," the name given to the rooms American GIs were tortured and abused in during the Korean War.

Leslie Orlikow, whose mother, Val, was brutally experimented on, including receiving 16 doses of LSD and electro-convulsive therapy that reduced her mind to that of a toddler (she was able to recover only after she left Allen and received sustained treatment from other therapists), reported that they only found out about Cameron's covert experimentation in 1977 when American congressional hearings exposed the man and his deeds. According to *The Scotsman* article, Orkilow stated that her mom thought Cameron was God—that he could do no wrong: "Then the researchers turned up that Cameron had been paid by the CIA for the mind control stuff, at which point my mother freaked out and was demoralized for a long time."

Their family received a $750,000 settlement from the CIA in 1988, but Val looked at it as dirty money, believing the CIA was not accepting any responsibility for the sleep room horrors she had been exposed to. Cameron no doubt ever accepted responsibility for the damage he caused to other human beings in his quest for control over the mind's innermost workings, something many experiment subjects can attest makes these men, and women, more monster than human. Is the desire to understand the human more important than the human as a whole? Clearly, the MKUltra program thought so, leaving behind a trail of broken victims and families struggling to understand how their own government could do such a thing.

Sometimes the enemy we most need to fear is the one that comes in the guise of a friend.

Note: Dr. Cameron was made president of the American Psychiatric Association in 1953. He was later made the first president of the World Psychiatric Association.

A Nation Betrayed

One of Cameron's victims, Carol Rutz, wrote an in-depth book about her own experiences as an MKUltra survivor: *A Nation Betrayed: The Chilling True Story of Secret Cold War Experiments Performed on Our Children and Other Innocent People*. Rutz documents her own journey as a victim from early childhood, along with her later quest for the truth via FOIA documents and extensive research into the men behind the experiments. She describes being literally handed over to the CIA at the age of 4 by her own grandfather in 1952, followed by years of tests, trainings, hypnosis, electroshock, drugs, sensory deprivation, and trauma "used to make me compliant and split my personality (create multiple personalities for specific tasks). Each alter of personality was created to respond to a post-hypnotic trigger, then perform an act and not remember it later."

Among those acts were giving sexual favors to high-ranking officials, spying, assassinations, and assisting in the abuse of other victims. Rutz was also a victim of other CIA programs, such as Bluebird and Artichoke, and her experiences were validated 48 years later with the release of more than 18,000 pages of declassified documents. Rutz mentions the creation of alters (alternate personalities), and this is something repeated by a number of MKUltra survivors who have hit the Internet as a means of spreading information about the projects. Alters could do what the main, or "front," personality would never agree to, and they would forget it all when it was over and done—the perfect tinker, tailor, soldier, spy.

"The following day," Rutz writes, explaining how one alter was created, "I was put in a white panel van with my little suitcase. (After arriving somewhere in Detroit) intense electroshock was delivered in order to allow my mind to dissociate and create Samantha who would never feel the pain. Samantha would automatically be the alter who took over the body. She would hide the memory and the pain from the rest of my system."

Children who experience extreme trauma and have no physical or psychological means of processing it, will split, and the MKUltra experimenters and handlers knew that they had the perfect medium with which to work in the malleable and innocent minds of a child. Rutz also writes about Dr. Cameron's experiment with her at the age of 12. She was given a shot of curare and put in a box in a converted stable behind the hospital that housed a behavioral lab. Snakes were put on top of her body and the lid was closed. Because of the curare, she could not move, and she was then exposed to taped programming via Dr. Cameron's famous "psychic driving" taped with trigger codes for what she claimed would be her own self-destruction. She writes, "This was done to prevent me from telling about the nature of this experiment in the event I would ever begin to remember."

When it came to programming alters, survivors speak of being exposed to more than one level of programming:

- **ALPHA:** General programming within the control personality.
- **BETA:** Sexual programming with child pornography, rape, prostitution, etc., eliminating all moral conviction so the sexual functions can be carried out without inhibition.
- **DELTA:** A sleeper assassin or trained killer. This level removes all fear and involves training with weapons and methods of killing and disposal of bodies.
- **THETA:** A form of psychic killing only used with subjects displaying a high level of ESP or psychic abilities.
- **OMEGA:** The self-destruct program installed in the event that a survivor remembers or tries to go public.

Rutz writes that this turned children "into warriors who would be the perfect Manchurian Candidates, perfect spies and assassins ignorant of their orders, fitting into society easily and anonymously, until a code is used to awaken them and send them into action."

Other MKUltra survivors tell of similar stories of ritual abuse, torture, even sexual abuse and pedophilia, often involving their own family members, many of whom are complicit in the torture and agreeable to selling their own children up the river for whatever sinister purposes their handlers have in mind. Some survivors speak of an association with black magic, Satanism, and occult practices. Others saw a link with secret societies such as the Freemasons, claiming the men who engaged in sex with children often were Masons. Others speak of high-level politicians and world leaders involved in the web of deception, abuse, and torture, including a few past presidents.

Though we have no physical proof of many of these claims, the very fact that so many survivors have similar stories, and the declassified documents back up that there indeed was an MKUltra, a BlueBird, an Artichoke, and even a Monarch, all suggest that we cannot brush these horrors under the rug. We know that prisoners in our own country and in others were and are tortured, especially those being detained on terrorism suspicions. Our own prisons, orphanages, and asylums have a dark history of allowing the most horrific and abusive experimentation to occur on those who had no power and could not fight back.

Unethical Research on Humans in the 20th Century
By Sarah N. Archibald, PhD

The 20th century saw great innovations when it came to science in general and medical advances in particular. Vaccines for many childhood diseases that were often lethal were developed, in addition to better ways of understanding the human body and to limit the deaths associated with the intervention of medical professionals.

Despite these innovations, there is also the dark shadow of questionable and downright unethical research conducted during the first three-quarters of the 20th century. Post–World War II highlighted some of the research issues on a global scale when the Nuremberg Trials took place. As part of the Nazis' defense for their barbaric research practices on those held in concentration camps, they argued that similarly unethical practices were taking place all over the world and specifically called the United States out in the use of prisoners for research experiments. The judges determined that there was no moral equivalence, and sentenced those on trial to long prison sentences or death.

However, the judges did note the need for ethical guidelines for human subjects research. These 10 principles outlined the elements needed to determine if an experiment should go forward, including minimizing risks and requiring informed consent. Unfortunately, the Nuremberg Code was not immediately adopted and questionable human subjects experimentation continued. In 1964, the Declaration of Helsinki was drafted and adopted by the World Medical Association. In particular, the group determined that "there be fair procedures and outcomes in the selection of research subjects."

The Nuremberg Code and the Declaration of Helsinki was not codified into U.S. law, which left the door open for researchers to experiment without any protections for human subjects. However, many experiments became public knowledge and led to an outcry by the public.

Most notable of these experiments is the Tuskegee Syphilis Study conducted by the National Institutes of Health (NIH). From 1932 until 1972, this study was designed to study the effects of untreated syphilis in a poor African-American community in Alabama. The participants were neither told of their diagnosis of syphilis nor treated for the disease, despite treatments becoming available in the 1940s. Hundreds of men were left untreated for a disease that could have been easily cured.

From 1955 until 1970, hepatitis experiments were conducted at the Willowbrook State School in Staten Island, New York, which served as a home for mentally disabled children. Hepatitis was a major health problem at the school and it was determined that measures needed to be taken to prevent infection. However, little was known about transmission of the disease, and it was not known at the time that there were two strains (A and B) that were prevalent at the school. In these experiments, newly admitted children were given protective antibodies in the hopes of preventing infection. They were then divided into two groups. One group would be injected with hepatitis while the other group would not (control group). Parents were given an informed consent document to sign and told they had to sign in order to allow their child to stay at Willowbrook. In 1963, the Jewish Chronic Disease Hospital Study was conducted. The researchers involved wanted to determine why the human body could not reject cancer cells. Without providing informed consent, 22 senile patients with chronic debilitating conditions were injected with live cancer cells to observe the transmission and bodily response to cancer. Luckily, these researchers were found guilty of fraud, something that rarely happened during this time period (post–World War II until the adoption of the Common Rule 45 CFR 46).

Despite the Nuremberg Code and the Declaration of Helsinki, the Unite States has a history (both before and after these guidelines were written) of experimenting on prisoners indiscriminately, without taking into account the risk to the prisoners and the repercussions of the experiments. "Two high[-]profile cases were the Oregon and Washington State prison radiation studies and the non-therapeutic biomedical research studies at Holmesburg Prison in Philadelphia" (Dober 2008). Experiments were conducted on prisoners in Pennsylvania up until the 1970s without the appropriate safeguards in place to protect the subjects. Multiple experiments were done on subjects at the same time, without controlling for the fact that there were other experiments being done on the same person. These experiments included the testing of skin products, drugs, and medical techniques. There have also been experiments done on those sentenced to death. In these cases, the prisoner was offered the "opportunity" to volunteer for the research and receive a life imprisonment sentence or a reprieve. One such prisoner was exposed to leprosy in a variety of ways and sent to the leper colony in Hawaii to determine the transmission of and progression of the disease. Another death row inmate "volunteered" to allow himself to be connected to a young girl dying of cancer, in order to have his blood go into the girl[…]to somehow filter out the cancer. The girl died despite this attempt. As a result of these experiments, and many more, the U.S. government decided to protect prisoners due to their lack of autonomy and the sometimes unscrupulous ways researchers used this population out of convenience.

In 1979, the Belmont Report was published; it called for re-spect for persons, beneficence, and justice. This report was ex-panded to the current regulations (45 CFR 46, also known as the Common Rule) in the late 1970s into the early 1980s. Due to the experiments noted here, among others, the U.S. Department of Health and Human Services included pregnant women (45 CFR 46 Subpart B), prisoners (45 CFR 46 Subpart C), and children (45 CFR 46 Subpart D) as vulnerable populations.

Sarah N. Archibald, PhD, is currently a research compliance specialist in the Human Research Protections Office the University of Maryland, Baltimore (UMB), and an adjunct assistant professor in the department of sociology at the University of Maryland, Baltimore County (UMBC). Dr. Archibald studies research ethics and various areas of criminology with an emphasis on capital punishment and inequality within the criminal justice system. She has a book coming out in early 2015 titled *Capital Punishment in U.S. States: Executing Social Inequality*?

Peter Lewis and his sister, Carol, were adopted from Germany in the 1950s. Now a survivor of MKUltra, Peter tells of his being "owned" by the U.S. Army. He recalled later that his adoptive mother allowed Peter to be given pills that caused him hallucinations and nightmares—most likely LSD—and often there were strange substances put into their cereal by doctors at Walter Reed Hospital. As a child, he was also subjected to radioactive experiments involving drinking radioactive material and then undergoing bone biopsies. This was done with him and other Boy Scouts he knew in 1958 at Walter Reed, where he and the other children were identified by numbers, not names. Peter's sister died of brain cancer from radiation experiments done 20 years earlier—the same time they were being exposed to the MKUltra program. At Vanderbilt University, from 1945 to 1949, pregnant women in the prenatal clinic were given a test substance to drink that they were told would be beneficial for their fetuses. They did not find out until later that the drinks contained a radioactive substance, resulting in several fatal malignancies.

Diet pills have been tested on children who were clinically classified as mentally retarded at Children's Center in Laurel, Washington, DC, and public school third graders were used to test the effects of

Nasal Radium Irradiation in experiments done by Johns Hopkins from 1948 to 1954.

The UFO Enigma

There is even a UFO angle involving MKUltra. In his book *Close Encounters of the Fatal Kind*, author/researcher Nick Redfern examines the links between the MKUltra agenda and UFO encounters. Redfern refers to Bosco Nedelcovic, a Yugoslavian who was employed in the 1950s by the U.S. Department of State's Agency for International Development (AID), during which time he worked on highly classified projects for the Department of Defense. Redfern writes:

> According to Nedelcovic, in the 1960s, secret elements of officialdom were engaged in the deliberate fabrication of UFO events using controversial methods similar to those that were born out of the CIA's MKUltra project that began in the 1950s.... That's to say, mind-altering cocktails, coupled with hallucinogenic drugs, were being used on unwitting members of the general public to convince them they had undergone encounters of the extraterrestrial variety when the reality was very different.

Redfern continues, stating there was a twofold agenda behind creating UFO events in the minds of men—and women. One was to determine how successfully the brain could be made to believe it had experienced something it had not, and two was "how to stage-manage faked, mind-manipulated events to try and figure out how the general populace might react to real encounters with extraterrestrials, should such entities one day appear en masse." Nedelcovic stated that plans were in place to fabricate UFO events in England and the United States between 1964 and 1965, and even told where they would be fabricated. One of those events was to occur at Exeter, New Hampshire. Interestingly, in 1965, a man named Norman Muscarello experienced just such a UFO event in Exeter, and a year later, a book called *Incident at Exeter* was published by journalist John J. Fuller, a man who had many links to mind control, MKUltra, and the death of Frank Olson—what was first claimed suicide, and later, a homicide. Fuller had been keyed in on the MKUltra mind control program in 1957, when he met with Dr. Karlis Osis and was given the chance for an inside look into the MKUltra program that some conspiracy theorists believe may also have been behind the famous Betty and Barney Hill UFO abduction in 1961, also in New Hampshire. Small world indeed.

Harvard Breeds a Bomber?

MKUltra employed the discreet services of dozens of facilities and universities, including Harvard University. During the fall of 1959, and all the way through to spring of 1962, 22 Harvard undergrad students were subjects in a series of experiments involving the use of extreme stress, emotional and verbal abuse, and behavior modification. Under the supervision of Henry Murray, a professor in the department of social relations and former director of the Harvard Psychological Clinic, who also happened to be part of the OSS, or Office of Strategic Services, and had during that time helped oversee military brainwashing experiments, conducted what critics later called unethical and even illegal experimentation at a location known as "The Annex," a house near the campus's department of molecular and cellular biology building. In this house, horrors took place on young students, including one 16-year-old named Theodore John Kaczynski, as Murray set out to measure how people react under stress by subjecting his subjects to intensive interrogation and verbal abuse, which Murray himself called "vehement, sweeping, and personally abusive" attacks, assaulting his subjects' egos and most-cherished ideals and beliefs.

Kaczynski later became known as the Unabomber. Could Murray's abusive experimentation perhaps have a role in subject's alienation and revenge against society? In an in-depth look at the Harvard experiments, "Harvard and the Making of the Unabomber," for The Atlantic in June 2000, reporter Alton Chase writes: "Such equivocation prompts one to ask, Could the experiment have had a purpose that Murray was reluctant to divulge? Was the multiform-assessments project intended, at least in part, to help the CIA determine how to test, or break down, an individual's ability to withstand interrogation?"

Though there is no direct proof that the Unabomber's years facing such experimentation and abuse had anything to do with his later behaviors and actions, it is possible that the brainwashing methods Murray employed on him and his fellow undergrads served to change his entire viewpoint and outlook, including his desire to later "leave civilization" and become alienated from the rest of the civilized world. Chase also writes: "I came to discover that Kaczynski is neither the extreme loner he has been made out to be nor in any clinical sense mentally ill. He is an intellectual and a convicted murderer, and to understand the connections between these two facts we must revisit his time at Harvard."

These are but a tiny drop in the bucket of the many studies and tests performed on people, including the mentally and physically challenged, imprisoned, pregnant, orphaned, and disabled, on behalf of the government, the military, pharmaceutical companies and corporations, and even private entities with an agenda. Why, then, should we doubt the stories of anyone claiming to have been brutally abused at the hands of our own CIA? One doctor who admits publicly of these experiments, even his own role in them, is Dr. G.H. Estabrooks, who described his own experimentation into creating multiple personalities in his books *Spiritism* and *Hypnotism*. Estabrooks claimed to create couriers and counterintelligence agents with hypnosis, as well as how to split certain individuals into complex personalities. He even experimented on children, corresponding with then FBI Director J. Edgar Hoover on various uses of hypnosis to interrogate juvenile delinquents.

Estabrooks called the creation of superspies and superassassins ethical because of the demands of war, but to those who were at the receiving end of the experimentation, there was nothing ethical about it. This rather unscrupulous attitude is what led to his own association with the same government agencies seeking themselves to achieve the ultimate warrior without a memory. The Manchurian Candidate.

If these mind control survivors are telling the truth, then the entire MKUltra period is one of the blackest marks on the evolution of humanity. Is it still going on, albeit under a different name and disguise? PSYOP, psychological warfare, is an accepted form of battle today. And someone has to try out all those new drugs big pharma is pumping out by the day.

From CIA document 17395, page 18:

> Learning models will be instituted in which the subject will be rewarded or punished for his overall performance and reinforced in various ways–by being told whether he was right, by being told what the target was, with electric shock, etc. In other cases, drugs and psychological tricks will be used to modify his attitudes. The experimenters will be particularly interested in dissociative states, from the abasement de niveau mental to multiple personality in so-called mediums, and an attempt will be made to induce a number of states of this kind, using hypnosis.

Your tax dollars at work.

Project Monarch: Fact or Fiction?
By Ron Patton

The 1990s were rife with sensational reports of satanic ritual abuse and a CIA mind control program involving the torture of children to create multiple personality disorder, or what is referred to today as dissociative identity disorder. Essentially, once the young victims were subjected to extreme and repetitive trauma, such as rape, electroshock, or witnessing horrific acts of violence, the mind would split into alters or personalities as a means to cope with the intense pain and shock.

Furthermore, these alters would be programmed with an assigned task or function, such as a drug courier, prostitute, assassin, human tape recorder, and so forth. Another way of examining this convoluted victimization is by looking at it as a complex computer program: A file (alter) is created through trauma, repetition, and reinforcement. In order to activate (trigger) the file, a specific access code or password (cue or command) is required. The name of this alleged sub-project of MKUltra, the CIA's notorious behavior modification program from the 1950s to 1970s, was known as Project Monarch.

There were 149 sub-projects listed under the auspices of MKUltra. Project Monarch has not been officially identified by any government documentation as one of the corresponding sub-projects, but is used rather, as a descriptive "catch phrase" by survivors, therapists, and possible "insiders." Monarch may in fact have culminated from MK-Search sub-projects such as Operation Spellbinder, which was set up to create "sleeper" assassins (i.e., "Manchurian Candidates") who could be activated upon receiving a key word or phrase while in a post-hypnotic trance.

Operation Often, a study that attempted to harness the power of occult forces, was possibly one of several cover programs to hide the insidious reality of Project Monarch. Of course, most skeptics would view this as simply a means to enhance trauma within the victim, negating any irrational belief that such supernatural or paranormal phenomenon actually occurs. Monarch programming is also referred to as the "Marionette Syndrome." "Imperial Conditioning" is another term used, and some mental health therapists know it as "Conditioned Stimulus Response Sequences."

The most notable purveyors of Monarch monomania were Mark Phillips and Cathy O'Brien, who co-wrote the book Trance Formation of America. This unsubstantiated autobiography contains compelling accounts of O'Brien's years of unrelenting incest and eventual indoctrination into Project Monarch by her father. Along with co-author Mark Phillips, a former CIA contractor and her supposed rescuer and deprogrammer, Cathy covers a sordid array of conspiratorial crime: forced prostitution (white slavery as a "Presidential Model") with those in the upper echelons of world politics and business, covert assignments as a "drug mule" and courier, and the country-western music industry and major league baseball connection with illegal CIA activities. To date, most of these allegations have not been validated or verified by credible sources.

Two other individuals proclaiming to have inside information relating to Project Monarch were Fritz Springmeier and

Cisco Wheeler. They co-wrote the voluminous and oddly named book The Illuminati Formula Used to Create an Undetectable Total Mind Controlled Slave. *It was ostensibly a mind control encyclopedia, saturated with detailed methods and techniques used for trauma-based programming. Springmeier (AKA Victor Schoof), a two-time convicted felon and self-proclaimed minister, played the role of rescuer and deprogrammer to alleged Monarch survivor Wheeler (AKA Linda Anderson). And like Phillips and O'Brien, much of the information disseminated was plausible, but the rest, speculative at best.*

Ted Gunderson, a former FBI agent, was also making unsubstantiated claims regarding satanic ritual abuse and the nefarious Project Monarch. He would embellish or exaggerate facts, and happened to be more publicly visible than the previous names mentioned, having appeared on numerous TV talk shows. Gunderson was usually pitted against Michael Aquino, former Army Lieutenant Colonel in psychological Wwrfare and founder of the Temple of Set, an offshoot of the Church of Satan. Aquino proposed there was no evidence of an organized satanic cabal who were kidnapping, torturing and sacrificing children. The end result of their seemingly contrived feud would usually leave the observer dazed and confused. Was this part of a dialectic used for containment? Could the proverbial "truth" be somewhere in the middle?

The False Memory Foundation, which began in 1992, was an organization that staunchly opposed recovered memory therapy, along with downplaying the existence of child sexual abuse. They believed many mental health practitioners were implanting memories through suggestion and hypnosis. However, this group was accused of misrepresenting the academic and scientific facts relating to memory. Their board of directors included Jolly West, an MKUltra doctor and Dr. Ralph Underwager, who advocated pedophilia. Were they part of the damage control to discredit claims of legitimate survivors of mind control and other related abuses?

Harlan Gerard, a political activist and whistle-blower, found no evidence or mention of a Project Monarch, prior to 1990.

H.P. Albarelli, an investigative journalist and author, also could not find proof of such a project occurring under the umbrella of MKUltra. Despite the fact there appeared to be individuals putting out sensational and dubious information about this heinous mind control project, there were a few MKUltra survivors and professionals in the fields of psychiatry and investigate journalism who had tenable explanations and writings about a trauma-based mind control program.

Dr. Corydon Hammond, a psychologist from the University of Utah, delivered a stunning lecture entitled "Hypnosis in MPD: Ritual Abuse" at the Fourth Annual Eastern Regional Conference on Abuse and Multiple Personality, on June 25, 1992, in Alexandria, Virginia. He confirmed the suspicions of the attentive crowd of mental health professionals, wherein a certain percentage of their clients had undergone mind control programming in an intensively systematic manner. Hammond alluded to the Nazi connection, military and CIA mind control research, and Greek letter and color programming, and specifically mentioned the Monarch Project in relation to a form of operative conditioning. He has since retracted from using the phrase "Project Monarch," but still believes in the premise of the programming.

New Orleans therapist Valerie Wolf introduced two of her patients before the President's Committee on Human Radiation Experiments on March 15, 1995, in Washington, DC. The astonishing testimony made by these women included accounts of German doctors, torture, drugs, electroshock, hypnosis, and rape, along with being exposed to an undetermined amount of radiation. Both Wolf and her patients stated they recovered the memories of this CIA program without regression or hypnosis.

Dr. Ellen P. Lacter, a highly respected psychologist in San Diego, California, has written extensive essays on the relationship between ritual abuse and trauma-based mind control programs. Another renowned psychologist, Dr. Colin A. Ross, wrote the groundbreaking book BLUEBIRD: Deliberate Creation of Multiple Personality by Psychiatrists. *This unparalleled work describes unethical experiments conducted by unscrupulous* psychiatrists to create amnesia, new identities, hypnotic access codes, and new memories in the minds of the experimental subjects. The end result was to create a Manchurian Candidate, or "super spy" who was multifaceted and, if captured, would not break under interrogation.

Kathleen Sullivan, an MKUltra victim, cogently wrote the startling book, Unshackled: A Survivor's Story of Mind Control. It's an account of her experiences as part of a criminal network that includes Intelligence personnel, military personnel, doctors, and mental health professionals contracted by the military and the CIA, criminal cult leaders and members, pedophiles, pornographers, drug dealers, and Nazis. She does recall a specific program installed into one of her alters or personalities, having to do with a monarch butterfly, prior to when the phrase "Project Monarch" became publicly recognized.

Another lucid MKUltra survivor, Carol Rutz, wrote the book A Nation Betrayed: Secret Cold War Experiments Performed on Our Children and Other Innocent People. What sets this book apart from other survivors' stories is it can be readily traced through declassified documents attained through the Freedom of Information Act. Rutz chillingly describes how, beginning at the age of 4, she was subjected to electroshock, drugs, hypnosis, sensory deprivation, and horrific trauma.

In retrospect, the Project Monarch era of the 1990s was a mix of hysteria and disinformation, congruent with confirmed accounts of such CIA mind control atrocities.

Ron Patton is a conspiracy researcher, writer, and executive producer of Paranoia TV on Tesla Wolf Media. He is also the owner of Paranoia: The Conspiracy Store in San Diego, California. He hosts Paranoia Radio, and has been a guest on numerous radio shows and podcasts. Patton is the executive producer of the annual Paranoia Con, an event featuring some of the world's most knowledgeable speakers, relating to conspiracy and the paranormal. Patton also published MKzine, a magazine examining coercive mind control, invasive human experimentation, and other related abuses.

Although the MKUltra era might have publicly been exposed, and ended, after the Senate hearings in the 1970s, most conspiracy and parapolitical theorists believe that the programs went deeper underground or continued into the 1990s under different names. And as we discuss in a future chapter, these methods of mind control seem crude compared to what is possible today, with technology lending a helping hand in the quest to control the thoughts and behaviors of others. In fact, by today's standards, shocking someone in a lab is prehistoric. Today, we can send a voice directly into the brain and make people do things they never would imagine doing.

As the next chapter suggests, though, even the more simple methods work just fine on the unsuspecting mind.

4

TRIGGERED: THE TOOLS AND TECHNIQUES OF CONTROL

The basic tool for the manipulation of reality is the manipulation of words. If you can control the meaning of words, you can control the people who must use the words.
—Philip K. Dick

If you don't control your mind, someone else will.
—John Allston

I don't really know what happened. I know I was there. They tell me I killed Kennedy. I don't remember what exactly I did, but I know I wasn't myself.
—Sirhan Sirhan

In order to achieve mastery and control over the thoughts and behaviors of another human being, a particular technique or tool comes in handy, especially if it serves to completely alter the existing personality and replace it with the desired personality. Mind control techniques can be subtle, and imperceptible to the one being controlled, but in many cases, the covert manipulation is done in a much more obvious, even ominous, manner.

Psychologist and author George K. Simon (*In Sheep's Clothing: Understanding and Dealing With Manipulative People*) wrote that to successfully manipulate another human being, a controller or abuser would have to 1) conceal his aggressive agenda and intentions; 2) know the psychological vulnerabilities of the intended victim, and modify the tactics accordingly; 3) be ruthless enough to not care if the victim is harmed; and 4) use covert aggression in the form of relational or passive-aggressive tactics. Knowing the weakness of the victim is paramount to achieving control, and many mind controllers have a sharp and keen eye for seeing those weaknesses early on and taking full advantage of them via a variety of means.

Reinforcement

One of the more subtle ways to make someone do what you want them to do uses reinforcement as both a tool and a weapon.

Positive reinforcement uses praise, flattery, admiration, attention, affection, gifts, charm, sexual desire, and declarations of love to create a sense of absolute adoration in the victim. This kind of technique is used by narcissists and psychopaths to secure a victim by what is called *"love-bombing,"* and setting the victim up on a pedestal for what will unfortunately be a brutal and abusive fall from grace once the desired outcome is achieved. Positive reinforcement is used in training dogs and horses, too, and does wonders compared to punishment. When used for the benefit of the individual, such as in giving positive praise to a child in school, or a training athlete, this kind of reinforcement can build confidence and self-esteem. Interestingly, its opposite also serves this same dual role of helping, and harming, the targeted individual.

Positive reinforcement is often used in cults, especially in the early stages of creating a bond between the cult leaders and members (more on cults in Chapter 7). This is also a popular way of bringing followers into a religious organization—by telling them they are "chosen" or "special" in the eyes of God—and serves to create an image that leaves no room for negative behaviors and attitudes. This can create a false sense of love, intimacy, and closeness that can, at times, depending on the motives, be turned against the victim later when abusive behavior rears its ugly head.

Negative reinforcement is the polar opposite, using punishment, criticism, and the silent treatment to manipulate the victim into a certain behavior. Negative reinforcement can include things like shaming, guilting, yelling, abusive language, and even physical violence to make someone behave. For a long time, we trained dogs with negative reinforcement, shoving their noses into their poo or slapping them on the nose if they did something wrong, until it was proven time and again that positive reinforcement worked better!

But in terms of human beings, using violence, fear, and virulent language serves as a strong means by which one can degrade, diminish, and dominate. Negative reinforcement would certainly include, at its extreme, torture and ritualistic abuse, which we will discuss more in detail later.

Yet, intriguingly, the most sinister form of this particular tool or technique involves the use of both positive and negative actions. **Intermittent reinforcement** is more devious and effective at creating such cognitive dissonance in the victims that they cannot help but surrender control to their abuser. Because intermittent reinforcement relies on doubt, fear, anxiety, expectation, and hope, it plays upon the deepest emotional needs of our humanity, and twists and turns them into an ugly display of trauma that can literally drive the victim insane, or to suicide.

It works like this: The controller/abuser uses positive reinforcement all the time in the beginning, setting the victim up to then crave more positive reinforcement, which is then taken away intermittently, to create confusion and anxiety. The victim wants more of what he got in the beginning, and begins to accept even negative reinforcement as long as it is peppered in with positive. At this point, the controller/abuser can begin to actually torture the victim, and the victim will become so desperate for the love and attention he once got, he will accept more and more periods of abuse and lack of positive enforcement. Soon, the victim is settling for crumbs of positive behavior from the controller/abuser, who now has the victim under complete control emotionally and physically.

Intermittent reinforcement can lead to obsession on the part of the victim, doing anything to get even a tiny bit of the positive reinforcement she was love-bombed with in the beginning. This is known as "traumatic bonding" in the field of psychology.

Covert forms of emotional manipulation serve to put the victim under a "spell" of sorts, because the damage is done on a subconscious level. Some victims claim later they did not even know they were being manipulated until it was too late, and they had been hooked in psychologically, becoming captives to a sick and dysfunctional individual bent on controlling and using them. Not only does this kind of manipulation change the behavior of the victim, it also changes his thoughts and perceptions, and his actual reality, and removes his individual will and power over time.

Lest anyone think that only stupid, weak, or desperate people become victims of this kind of manipulation, the easiest victims are actually empathic, compassionate people of all levels of intellect. Controllers seem to know how to zero in on those who have big, trusting hearts, which is often why children are used in mind control experiments and ritual abuse. Extremely intelligent people join cults. It has nothing to do with how smart a person is, and everything to do with how trusting, caring, and open he is—which makes him a perfect target for manipulators all along the spectrum. Psychopaths will actually seek out empathic people for abuse, as will narcissists, both masters at mind control.

Coercive Persuasion

This works along the same lines, using destructive mind control tools that serve to take away an individual's control. Steven Alan Hassan, a licensed counselor and former member of the Unification Church, now operates the Freedom of Mind Center, to research and assist people who need deprogramming from mind control cults. Hassan stated in *Coercive Persuasion, Mind Control and Brainwashing*, in an interview with author Liane Leedom, MD, in 2007, that "destructive mind control takes the 'locus of control' away from the individual." It does so by using four basic tactics to systematically manipulate and alter the individual's identity, to which he gave the acronym BITE: behavior, information, thoughts, and emotions.

Behavioral modification can include telling a person how to dress, act, worship, look, eat, sleep, have sex, and so on. The idea is to, over time, control behavior and foster a dependency upon the controller/abuser. Autonomy no longer exists.

Information is controlled and selectively given to the victim, to alter her perceptions and reality. Thoughts and emotions are governed with an iron fist. Victims are not permitted to think for themselves, and show of emotion is frowned upon, if not outright punished. The use of fear, shame, and guilt can play a large role in shaping a person's mind, or changing it, especially the fear of physical harm and/or death. That is why torture serves as a great tool to make someone confess—even to a crime he or she did not commit. Taking away food, water, sleep, access to information, exposure to light, and a host of other physical forms of deprivation, coupled with psychological manipulation, can turn the toughest person to mush.

When it comes to these brainwashing techniques, there is a much slower and more systematic approach to dismantling a victim's will and identity than in outright torture or physical violence. Dr. Margaret Singer, a clinical psychologist and anti-cultist who focused her career studies on brainwashing, cults, and coercive persuasion used in mind control, writes in an article for F.A.C.T.Net.com titled "Coercive Mind Control Tactics": "Coercive psychological systems are behavioral change programs which use psychological force in a coercive way to cause the learning and adoption of an ideology or designated set of beliefs, ideas, attitudes, or behaviors." Singer listed a number of tactics used to create these psychological changes, which work both on an individual and on a social group/society:

Increase Suggestibility: Uses audio, visual, and verbal suggestibility-increasing stimuli, even hypnosis, sleep deprivation, and restricting water and food.

Establish Control Over Social Environment and Support: Uses rewards and punishments including social isolation, abridged contact with family/friends, builds dependence on controller/cult/abuser.

Prohibit Disconfirming Information: Disallows any opinions or outside information that goes against the motives and agendas of the controller/cult/abuser.

Force Re-Evaluation of a Person's Aspects of Experience of Self: Destabilizes and undermines a victim's conscious awareness of individual reality, worldview, emotional control, and even defense mechanisms. A new life history and reality is instilled.

Create Powerlessness: Subjects victims to intense, frequent actions that undermine their confidence and judgment.

Create Aversive Emotional Arousal: Uses non-physical methods of punishment to change emotions and behavior, including shaming, guilting, and social isolation.

Intimidate: Threaten the victim with the force of group-sanctioned threats that will lead to certain punishments if the victim does not go along or adopt the controller's attitudes, beliefs, and so forth.

Obviously, the more severe and extreme these tactics are utilized, the more control the victim gives up. Victims suffer in a perpetual state of confusion and chaos, even PTSD (post-traumatic stress disorder), even after they get away from the controllers and sources of abuse, leaving them with symptoms such as severe depression, anxiety and panic attacks, insomnia, physical illness, emotional debilitation, inability to concentrate and focus, and a host of other ailments. Yes, long after a person is no longer in the grips of a controlling person or entity, the control continues, often driving the person to suicide, insanity, or psychiatric care if proper help and support aren't found.

Rhetoric and Dogma

Two of the most pervasive methods of controlling other people come in the form of language and belief, and when paired together create some of the most dangerous religious extremism. Rhetoric and dogma are the twisted sisters of cults, too, which seek to disempower their members and change their entire identities and belief systems as a means to keep them in line with the desire of the leader/leaders.

Rhetoric is an art form designed to use argument and discourse to convince others of our point of view, of our beliefs. Ancient Greek philosophers studied rhetoric as a cooperative form of communication that involved three "rhetoric appeals" to change another person's belief:

1. **Logos:** The use of logical argument and induction/deduction.
2. **Pathos:** The use of creating emotional reaction in the listener(s).
3. **Ethos:** The projection of an image of trustworthiness, authority, and charisma.

The balance of logic, emotion, and trust, along with a dose of magnetic charisma, serves to create an honest and open discussion of disagreements. But, as with most anything, there is a dark side. Rhetoric has been absconded by political, religious, and cult leaders eager to persuade their followers to stand in line with a particular set of beliefs and behaviors, to accept their *dogma*, which is a set of principles accepted as truths by authority figures. Dogma is the foundational basis of any system of belief or ideology, the very paradigm of that ideology itself, and rhetoric is one of the many tools by which dogma is imposed upon those who need to stay within the confines of that given paradigm. Dogma has a negative connotation to most people because of its association with religion and politics, which force followers or adherents to accept a particular opinion or point of view, even when it does not serve their best interest. Mind control at its finest. If you can use the right tools to actually get people to join your church or vote for you, even when it harms them, you've got them by the balls, and the brains.

It is rhetoric, used by the most charismatic of figures, that whips people into a frenzied state of emotionally charged submission, whereby they more easily absorb and accept the dogma attached to that rhetoric. Adolf Hitler was a master at the use of words to persuade people to change their beliefs, beyond any debate or disagreement they might have initially felt at his suggested dogma. Millions died as the result of this potent combination.

Capture Bonding/Stockholm Syndrome

The shift from brutal tactics alternated with less invasive and abusive ones, to create confusion and total disorder of the thought processes in the victims, also served another purpose: This alternating of tactics, similar to someone who is exposed to an extremely abusive spouse who at times is gentle and loving, often works even better than straight, non-stop, hard-core abuse, because the victim comes to almost be thankful to the captors for the "gentle" moments. It leads to "capture bonding," better known as Stockholm Syndrome.

POWs and hostages during wartime sometimes develop positive feelings toward—even allegiance to—their captors when this tactic is used. A lack of abuse after a long period of having to deal with physical and psychological torture is seen as an act of kindness on behalf of the captors/abusers and creates an emotional tie to the captor. The victim now sees the captor, when kindness is made available, as a kind of savior. But the ego also plays a role in this phenomenon. After being abused for so long, a victim may develop Stockholm Syndrome as a coping mechanism or a defensive system. It may also serve as an adaptive measure in our evolution, for times when our ancestors were abducted, kidnapped, or conquered by other warring tribes and nations. If the captives fought back or rebelled, they and their families might die, so by forming some kind of bond with the enemy, they kept themselves alive a little longer, and often ended up joining their captors or at least avoided being killed by them.

Sometimes, the abused goes so far as to even join the abusers in their cause, and switches allegiance to the motives, agendas, and belief systems of the enemy camp.

The name "Stockholm Syndrome" comes from a 1973 bank robbery in Norrmalmstrog, in Stockholm, Sweden, where bank employees were held hostage in a bank vault for six days. The standoff went on as the robbers negotiated with the police, but during the crisis, the employees formed an emotional attachment to the robbers, even saw them as being right in their actions against the Swedish government, and defended their own captors' actions when freed after a six-day ordeal.

The exact opposite occurs as well, when a captor becomes emotionally bonded to their hostage or hostages. This is called Lima Syndrome, named after a hostage crisis in Lima, Peru, in 1996 when a militant group took hundreds of people hostage during a party for a Japanese ambassador and later freed most of the hostages, allegedly after developing empathy and sympathy for them.

Most of us think we will never have to experience such a strange attachment, but psychologists point to relationships between narcissists/sociopaths and co-dependents as a similar and more widely experienced version of the captor–captive bond. Mind control is more a part of our psychological tendencies than we might care to admit.

In *How Full Is Your Bucket?* authors Tom Rath and Donald O. Clifton, PhD, looked at the treatment of POWs during the Korean War, focusing on the studies of U.S. Army chief psychiatrist Major William E. Mayer. Mayer studied more than 1,000 American POWs who were detained in a North Korean camp, looking for the most extreme cases of psychological warfare on record. What he found was that these POWs were not tortured or abused physically much, and were given food, water, and shelter. They were not detained under particularly cruel conditions, and they were not even detained in these camps by armed guards or barbed wire fences!

Why then, did the suicide rate among these POWs climb to 38 percent? And why did half of the dying admit they had simply "given up"?

Mayer determined that the cause of this was "extreme hopelessness," which came from emotional abuse of the worst kind, the kind that made these men lifeless and psychologically debilitated, even those that were later rescued. The objective of the North Koreans was to "deny men the emotional support that comes from interpersonal relationships." Using isolation, withholding of positive support, criticism, and malicious negativity, including the withholding of letters the soldiers would receive from loved ones at home, the captors were able to destroy the victims' from the inside out: "The soldiers had nothing to live for and lost basic belief in themselves and their loved ones, not to mention God and country. The North Koreans had put the American soldiers into a kind of emotional and psychological isolation, the likes of which have never been seen."

This kind of brainwashing, mind control, and behavioral modification is terrifying, because it is something many of us will experience to some degree in our own lifetimes dealing with narcissists, sociopaths, and psychopaths—and we may not know what hit us until we are depressed, despondent, and destroyed. The good news is, once we recognize the manipulative tactics themselves, we can do something about it and stop the devastating effects on our minds, psyches, and souls.

Ritual Abuse, and Programming Cues and Triggers

Perhaps the most terrifying and shocking methods by which one can control the mind and behaviors of another are ritual abuse and torture. Torture-based mind control is often associated with ritual abuse, sometimes linked with satanic rituals and secret societies involved with heinous practices against children, including rape and sacrifice. This kind of extreme and ongoing abuse often begins in childhood, and may or may not be associated with a government program, as in the MKUltra program discussed in the previous chapter. Sometimes, alleged victims claim that family dynasties and lineages are involved in a sort of generation abuse that may take on the guise of a secret society. Other victims claim the military or powerful corporate entities were the abusers.

The idea behind this kind of abuse might be to create a super soldier, an assassin, or a spy, but sometimes it was simply part of a ritual practice with no external motivation other than that of the members involved in the ritual. This is said to be a global phenomenon, with victims from several countries reporting secret government-sponsored mind-control programs. Many of the victims are under the age of 18 and do not give their own consent. A parent or guardian, however, may not only give consent, but be an abuser or working with the abusers. Some survivors even link organized crime entities to this kind of ritualistic torture and abuse.

Adult survivors of childhood ritual abuse report that they were threatened with death if they told about their abuse, according to "Torture-Based Mind Control as a Global Phenomenon," which documents preliminary data from a 2007 series of Extreme Abuse Surveys (EAS) and was presented by W. Karriker at the 13th International Conference on Violence, Abuse and Trauma in 2008. Among the statistics reported:

- Of the 257 EAS respondents who reported that secret mind control experiments were used on them as children, 69 percent, or 177 people, reported abuse in a satanic cult.
- 93 percent of professionals who responded to the related question had worked with at least one survivor who had been threatened with death if he or she talked about the abuse.
- 67 percent of 218 professionals who responded to the related question have worked with at least one client who reported electroshock abuse.
- 50 percent of adult survivors who responded to the related question reported electroshock abuse.

Aside from these statistics, the data showed percentages of "memories installed by their perpetrators," or installed programming, including:

- Use of blood in abuse.
- Starvation.
- Brain stimulation.
- Prostitution.

- ○ Forced drugging.
- ○ Sensory deprivation.
- ○ Witnesses animal mutilations/slaughter.
- ○ Being caged.
- ○ Being forced to abuse other victims.
- ○ Bondage.
- ○ Spinning.
- ○ Sexual abuse by multiple perpetrators.
- ○ Microwave abuse.
- ○ Radiation exposure.
- ○ UFO abduction.
- ○ Dislocation of limbs.
- ○ Pornography.
- ○ Injection of painful eye drops.
- ○ Incest.

Sadly, that is only a partial sampling of the memories reported by alleged victims. One of the major outcomes of this kind of extreme abuse is the diagnosis of DID, or dissociative identity disorder (multiple personalities/alters), in victims. Sadistic abuse splits the personality, a coping mechanism designed to protect the real personality by allowing others to step in and cope with the horror and physical trauma. These alters can also be programmed to perform crimes, murder, assassinations, and other activities that the original personality would never agree to, or possibly even be capable of. Each alter is separate and distinct from the original personality, which is called the *front personality*, but can also be aspects of the front personality. For many with DID, the front personality has no clue of the alters' existence. Many people will remember the movie *Sybil*, with a young Sally Field playing Shirley "Sybil" Mason, a woman who spent most of her adult life in psychotherapy with a Dr. Cornelia Wilbur (played by Joanna Woodward) in an attempt to identify and merge her 16 various personalities, said to be the result of extreme emotional trauma. Despite the controversy over whether or not Mason was really suffering from multiple personalities or not, the disorder is real and something many victims of systematic ritual abuse experience.

In *Hell Minus One*, Anne Johnson-David recounts her horrible experiences being sexually, physically, and mentally abused by her own parents, as part of a satanic ritual. What makes her story even more powerful is that her parents confessed their abuse to local clergymen and detectives with the Utah Attorney General's Office, who found evidence of ritual abuse after spending $250,000 and three years investigating the claims. They could not, however, prosecute at the time. The abuse began when Anne was 3 years old and continued until she ran away from home at the age of 17. She was drugged, tortured, symbolically sacrificed, painted with blood, and even forced to harm her own siblings during satanic rituals. Her memories of the abuse were suppressed until she was in her mid-30s, when they erupted into her conscious mind and were later corroborated by her own abusers—her parents.

But her story is not singular. Many ritual abuse survivors have come forward to tell their stories, such as Jeanne Adams, author of *Childhood Ritual Abuse* and *Drawn Swords*. Adams wrote in "I Am Many: Profiling the Ritual Abuse Survivor," in the Winter 2004 *MKzine*, "We are finding each other, organizing and healing." Adams advocates for survivors and their healing, as well as educating professionals to identify and understand ritual abuse and the surrounding issues faced by those who suffer long into their adult years.

Adams did her own research, surveying abuse survivors to find common links and characteristics of the abuse. One of her findings concluded that the most often reported age when childhood abuse comes into the conscious awareness of the adult survivor is between ages 30 and 40, with the second highest occurring between ages 40 and 50. In many cases, the abuse is so traumatic, the mind successfully blocks it until the person is older and more mature, and hopefully able to cope with the revelations and implications.

Unfortunately, as with rape and sexual assault victims, the victims of childhood ritual abuse are often blamed for what was done to them, called crazy, or said to be out for money and publicity. Often these victims are told they have *false memory syndrome*.

False Memory Syndrome

Often in a therapy setting, people who claim they were sexually or physically abused during childhood may have a difficult time remembering actual details of the abuse. The brain has a way of shaping memory based on perceptions, expectations, and worldviews, all of which change as we become adults. False memory syndrome is described as a condition in which a person's identity and personal relationships center on memories of traumatic experiences that may not have actually happened, but that the person truly *believes* did. Once a memory is entrenched, the brain becomes attached to that memory in a way that literally dictates the person's life and identity, and is resistant to correction.

This controversial syndrome or condition (this is not a recognized mental condition within the psychiatric community) can be created during actual therapy, where thoughts of abuse are suggested or implanted as seeds in the brain's hippocampus, thus triggering memories, as vague and blurred as they might be, of potential events that may corroborate the suggested or planted thoughts. The brain has a wonderful way of seeking out what it wants to, and often someone who claims to have experienced childhood trauma is accused of "creating" the trauma from reading self-help books, seeking therapy, listening to other alleged victims, and identifying with them, despite no actual proof any abuse did occur in his or her distant past.

Memory is often tainted by time, distance, and perception, and it becomes almost impossible, without further proof of other witnesses or physical evidence, that abuse did occur in the way the adult survivor remembers it. But that is not to say these survivors are lying or making things up—because in many cases they do have corroborating evidence, even confessions of the abusers themselves, photographs, videotapes, other eyewitnesses, and so on. This is not a black and white subject by any means.

One of the most famous criminal cases that involved the allegations of false memory syndrome was the McMartin preschool trial. During the 1980s, we experienced what some call a Satanic panic, when the news was filled with allegations of sexual abuse during satanic rituals and gatherings, many involving children. The McMartin family, who operated a preschool in California, was charged in 1983 with 321 acts of sexual abuse of children who were their care. From 1984 to 1987, a number of arrests were made, including Virginia McMartin, Peggy Mc-Martin Buckey, Ray Buckey, Ray's sister Peggy Ann Buckey, and teachers Mary Ann Jackson, Betty Raidor, and Babette Spitler. There were no actual convictions and all charges were dropped in 1990, making it the longest and most expensive criminal trial in American history.

To this day, there are those who believe actual abuse did occur, but because the victims were children, there was not enough solid evidence to know who exactly committed what acts. In some cases, as adults, a few of the children involved retracted their accusations. Whether or not these children were abused, and with all of the sexual abuses we hear about on a daily basis, this would not be unheard of, and it became lost in the accompanying media whirlwind of "satanic" allegations that overshadowed and may have even influenced the outcome.

S.M.A.R.T. Responses

Every summer, Neil Brick, editor of a newsletter devoted to ritual abuse and mind control, *S.M.A.R.T. (Stop Mind Control and Ritual Abuse Today)*, hosts a conference in Connecticut called "The Ritual Abuse, Secretive Organization and Mind Control Conference." Devoted to speakers and presentations involving mind control and abuse, various cues and triggers are presented that survivors have experienced. In "How Cues and Programming Work in Mind Control and Propaganda," Brick's presentation in May 2003, he stated:

> Many triggers or cues are innate. An example of a trigger or cue could be a hot feeling when going near an oven burner. Almost instinctively, a person would pull their hand away from the burner. This would be an unconditioned response. There are conditioned and unconditioned triggers or stimuli and conditioned or unconditioned responses. Pavlovian classical conditioning involves pairing an unconditioned stimuli with a conditioned stimuli to get a conditioned response.

For those who are survivors of ritual or torture-based mind control, the programming they are exposed to works in similar fashions, with the creation of conditioned responses to various stimuli. Sometimes, a survivor will be tortured on a repeated basis to the point where an alter, or alternate personality, is created, and the alter then is given a cue to let it know when to come out. It could be a particular word, phrase, smell, sound, or number that then triggers the alter to appear. "The law of strength applies to the strength of the trauma and the strength of the cue," Brick writes. "A stronger smell may be easier to associate with a strong trauma, which makes the conditioning stronger. Also if the alter and cue are paired together or closer in terms of time, they will associate more easily."

Though it is frightening to think that we are being exposed to such Pavlovian tactics, advertisers do the same thing when trying to hook us into buying their product. More on that later, but remember: Mind control tools are not always reserved for the most secretive and conspiracy-laden programs. They can be done to anyone at any time. Brick writes: "Propaganda techniques are similar in many ways to programming techniques. One could say a person is being programmed when being propagandized. The combination of vision and sound on TV make a person more suggestible."

Ritual abuse survivors experience the worst kind of these tools and tactics, though, because for many of them the abuse begins in early childhood and involves the most extreme forms of physical and mental torture. Even if a ritual abuse survivor gets help as an adult, PTSD is common, as are the shame and fear of having to face what happened to them, sometimes at the hands of people they knew and trusted. Whereas we all are programmed to perform certain behaviors to gain approval from others, survivors of ritual abuse perform certain behaviors often unwillingly, unknowingly, and from a deep subconscious reaction to cues and triggers they may not even be aware of, or remember when they are older.

Neil Brick suggests ways that victims can extricate themselves from the grip of mind control in "Survivor Tactics," in the Winter 2004 issue of *MKZine*:

○ Watch less or no TV. Television puts us in a brainwave state that makes us all suggestible to subliminal programming.

○ Break addictions. Addictions may be used as a crutch or coping method for survivors, but keep victims from processing the trauma fully and moving on.

○ Find a spiritual system. First make sure we are free of cult or religious programming, and then find a spiritual system that works for us.

○ See the truth about our political system(s). Being aware of the corruption and how the media and government work together, one can then begin to think for him- or herself, and not be influenced or under government control.

○ Never give up. Recovering from mind control abuse can take decades, but freedom of mind can be achieved with hard work and time. Have a voice. Refuse to compromise if it means another child or person will be abused or brainwashed.

Kathleen Sullivan wrote first-hand about her experiences with mind control and the traumatic ritual abuse she was exposed to as an MKUltra victim and at the hands of her own family, as well as an organized network of Satanists, occultists, Aryans, military and intelligence personnel, and members of secret societies such as the Freemasons, in her book, Unshackled: A Survivor's Story of Mind Control. *Here, she discusses how survivors can recover from such abuse, programming and manipulation, and how the public, by opening their minds and hearts to these survivors, can help in the process.*

Welcome Them Home
By Kathleen Sullivan

One of my favorite recovery models is the Johari Window, originally developed by Joseph Luft and Harry Ingham in 1955. On paper, the model—which looks like a four-paned window—represents four kinds of human self-awareness and consciousness.

Here are the four parts of the window:

○ Open area *(top left-hand quadrant) represents the part(s) of ourselves that we are consciously aware of, and so are others.*

○ Blind area *(top right-hand quadrant) represents the part(s) of ourselves that others are aware of, but we are not.*

○ Hidden area *(bottom left-hand quadrant) represents the part(s) of ourselves that we consciously know about, but others don't.*

○ Unknown area *(bottom right-hand quadrant) represents the part(s) of ourselves that neither we nor others consciously know about.*

One of the reasons so many intelligent criminals successfully hide their illegal activities from our conscious awareness is that they know how to identify and manipulate our society's blind areas. They know, sometimes better than we do, what we are willing to tolerate knowing and what we prefer not to become consciously aware of.

Our society's blind areas are where such perpetrators generally operate—individually and collectively. They are right in believing that few of us will even notice our society's blind areas until another investigator, researcher, or survivor shines a bright light of solid truth to expose it.

In a similar way, we all have personal blind areas. It usually takes a lot of strength, courage, and resolve for any person to voluntarily explore the darkest blind areas of his or her own life or past.

It takes even more courage for most mind control survivors to self-explore, because most of them have already been forced, coerced, or blackmailed to commit sins and crimes that seem so horrendous or unforgiveable that the survivors understandably prefer to keep the awareness of them hidden in their own blind areas.

Because most survivors carry deep, hidden wounds and scars from such encounters with extreme human evil, they usually need larger amounts of aid and support from our society to heal and recover. Unfortunately, most survivors recoil—at least at first—from that help because they fear that the helpers will find the hidden "evil" in them and eventually reject them.

Most survivors of trauma-based mind control have already survived extreme amounts of pain, betrayal, and more. They've instinctively figured out how to numb their minds, hearts, and bodies to protect and keep themselves alive. They also instinctively sense that they can literally die if they open their hearts or thaw out their numbness and try to accept love and caring from the outside world.

They know that if they open up to love and caring, and then they are rejected, it will simply prove what the abusers already taught them: that they are evil, damaged goods, a plague, unworthy of regular society's—and their higher power's—purer forms of love and acceptance.

Unfortunately, because the survivors' trauma histories are unusually hard-core, fewer people have the capacity to open their hearts to them and learn about what they've already suffered at the hands of seriously dangerous psychopaths.

Survivors whose traumatic histories are rejected also are more likely to take such a natural defensive reaction as a rejection of themselves. They may not yet understand that the rejection is the listener's or reader's way of protecting the mind and heart from information that threatens his or her belief that the world is a safe place.

In the not so distant past, too many survivors of trauma-based mind control told me that after leaving their abusers, they eventually went back to them—at least for a while—because when the survivors tried to tell outside people about their traumas, their stories were rejected.

The survivors then made a willful choice to go back to their abusers because, at least from them, the survivors knew what kind of pain to expect. They already knew how to numb their minds and bodies to torture, sexual brutalization, psychological assaults, and more. They already knew how to cope with that kind of devastating pain.

What they couldn't bear was to experience rejection from decent, caring people whom they had dared to open their hearts and minds to in deeply personal ways.

That was then; this is now. Today, more survivors of trauma-based mind control are receiving validation and support from the greater world, which is waking up more and more to the existence of such atrocities. This also means that more survivors are receiving solid aid and support to survive, heal, and recover.

But there are still other truths that haven't been told. Many survivors of trauma-based mind control are still keeping that information safe in the "hidden areas" of their conscious awareness. They still have valid fears that if those other secrets are also told, the survivors may still be rejected. This is tragic, because they also do not yet feel safe enough to tell us about the many unusual strengths, skills, gifts, and abilities that were forged in the dark fires of humanly created hells.

Their unique gifts are now available to all of us, if we will dare to open our hearts and accept them. All we really have to do, to move forward in our collective process of societal healing, is to sit down with open hearts and listen to the survivors who still need to share the rest of their stories.

By the simple act of listening with open and accepting hearts, we will send them the signal for which many have been waiting for, some for decades. And in turn, they will share their beautiful gifts with us.

Hopefully, this book will encourage us to send that strong signal to them. It's time for us to prove to them that our modern society is strong, brave, and caring. It's time for us to face and accept our collective blind areas, make the hidden information open and available, and validate the secrets still carried by the disenfranchised refugees. It's time for us to welcome them home.

Hypnosis

One of the most widely used and reported modes of controlling another person's mind and behavior involves hypnosis. Most people don't know that the word *hypnosis* comes from the Greek word for "sleep," *hypnos*, but true hypnosis is not sleep at all. It is an altered state of awareness characterized by the ability to intensely focus on a memory or past event, a sort of pseudo-sleep where the person is actually awake, but in a different mental state than normal conscious awareness. People under hypnosis are not zombies, but are highly suggestible. Aside from the entertainment-based hypnosis shows, which are, of course, done for show, true hypnosis is a subtle way of influencing a human mind, without overtly subjecting it to direct brainwashing or abuse.

When one is induced into a hypnotic state, usually in a therapeutic setting, with a desire to overcome a phobia or give up smoking or a bad health habit, the mind is aware of its surroundings and remains in control, yet is also open to suggestions and able to access memories in a much sharper, more defined manner than during the normal waking state. A new definition of hypnosis was presented in 2005, by the Society for Psychological Hypnosis, Division 30 of the American Psychological Association (APA):

> Hypnosis typically involves an introduction to the procedure during which the subject is told that suggestions for imaginative experiences will be presented. The hypnotic induction is an extended initial suggestion for using one's imagination, and may contain further elaborations of the introduction. A hypnotic procedure is used to encourage and evaluate responses to suggestions. When using hypnosis, one person (the subject) is guided by another (the hypnotist) to respond to suggestions for changes in subjective experience, alterations in perception, sensation, emotion, thought or behavior. Persons can also learn self-hypnosis, which is the act of administering hypnotic procedures on one's own. If the subject responds to hypnotic suggestions, it is generally inferred that hypnosis has been induced. Many believe that hypnotic responses and experiences are characteristic of a hypnotic state. While some think that it is not necessary to use the word "hypnosis" as part of the hypnotic induction, others view it as essential.

The use of hypnosis has been linked to MKUltra experiments to create alternate personalities that are capable of killing someone, having sex, committing crimes, and other activities that would be unbeknown to the front personality, and only accessed when the person is put into a hypnotic state. Cults allegedly use hypnotic language to draw in members, inducing a state of suggestibility that allows for very intelligent members of society to turn their lives, and finances, over to a charismatic cult leader.

In a transcript of a speech given by Dr. Corydon Hammond, a psychologist, professor, and author involved in mind control, cults, and ritual abuse research, titled "Cults, Ritual Abuse and Mind Control: Exploring the Role of Cults in Ritual Abuse and Mind Control," Hammond is stated as saying, "The way you create a Manchurian Candidate is you divide the mind. It's part of what the intelligence community wanted. If you're going to get an assassin, you divide the mind." Hammond points out that assassin Sirhan Sirhan, who killed Robert F. Kennedy, had total amnesia when examined by courtroom psychiatrist Bernard Diamond. Yet when put under hypnosis, Sirhan could remember killing Kennedy, and only under hypnosis could he recall anything about the event. When it comes to children, Hammond stated:

> What they basically do in these programs is they get a child and start programming in basic forms, it appears, by about age two and a half, after the child's already been made dissociative. They'll make him dissociative not only through abuse, like sexual abuse, but also things like putting a mousetrap on their fingers and teaching the parents, "You do not go in until the child stops crying. Only then do you go in and remove it." They start in rudimentary forms at about age two and a half and kick into high gear, it appears, around six or six and a half. They continue through adolescence with periodic reinforcements in adulthood.

With this kind of hypnotic programming so early in life, by the time the victims are adults, they are so programmed, they may not even own their own mind anymore. Cues and triggers are used to activate the alters into performing a murder or crime or sex act during a ritual, and the front personality may never know what happened. Using hypnosis combined with abuse seems to be the perfect recipe for breaking down a human into a subservient, controlled machine, with body, mind, and spirit shattered and reprogrammed for the agendas of others, no matter how sinister.

In 1968, H.D. Birns, author of several books on hypnosis, writes in "Hypnosis" how a personality is deliberately split: "The starting place to deliberately create a manageable multiple personality is, of course, with a normal person who has a self-controlled conscious and a self-controlled unconscious. The next step is to displace the conscious will, substituting it with the will of the hypnotist. That goal would require achieving a very deep state of hypnosis with the subject."

Birns goes on to compare a hypnotist who has complete control of a subject to a "driver operating an automobile," stressing the powers of the hypnotist to truly control the subject.

With many layers and levels of programming reported by ritual abuse and mind control survivors, there is often a sense of no longer having a true identity or if one does exist, it is so buried beneath a pile of programs that one cannot easily access it. Sometimes, the true identity is purposely blocked from ever being accessed, which would make it much easier to keep a programmed assassin from ever waking up and smelling the coffee, and being able to possibly upset the balance of power by whistle-blowing.

Thus the alleged links between assassinations and hypnotic programming. Take a patsy, program him to kill an important public figure, create such a strong alter that his true identity never even knows the reality of the situation unless under hypnosis, and you have the perfect soldier, spy, killer. Maybe that is why chief psychologist at San Quentin Prison in 1969, Dr. Eduard Simson-Kallas, while examining Sirhan Sirhan with his colleague Dr. David G. Schmidt, chief psychiatrist at the prison, concluded that Sirhan was not schizophrenic, or psychotic, and was indeed a very good hypnotic subject. In fact, according to a court affidavit, Simson-Kallis believed Sirhan was programmed to kill Kennedy: "He was put up.... He would be easily blamed, being an Arab. He was programmed to be up there."

As the previous chapter shows, working with the Nazis after World War II through the Cold War era and into more modern times, our own government and military experimented with hypnosis and mind control for various purposes. One of those purposes was to create assassins. In

Secret, Don't Tell: The Encyclopedia of Hypnotism, Carla Emery fully and comprehensively documents the use of hypnosis throughout the history of mind control, most notably during the CIA's various projects, including MKUltra. She lays out the goals of various CIA programs, one of which stated that the use of "hypnotic memory training" was more like "memory enhancement," which uses hypnosis to make an existing memory stronger and better. This kind of memory enhancement, Emery notes, was used for two specific goals in government and military backed mind control:

1. To create couriers bearing unconsciously remembered messages.
2. Subjects used as human tape recorders where no mechanical recording of speech was possible or permitted.

In the case of Project Bluebird, the goal was to achieve the absence of resistance and counter-control, and all done in a way that the subject wouldn't even know he or she was being manipulated. This statement from the CIA memo, "Defense Against Soviet Medical Interrogation and Espionage Techniques" sums it up: "Hypnotism would make it possible to brief a prisoner or other individual, subsequently dispatch him on a mission and successfully debrief him on his return without his recollection of the whole proceeding."

Perfect little soldiers.

Shooter Syndrome?

Because the use of hypnosis has been linked to CIA projects involving mind control, detailed in Chapter 3, people have wondered if recent tragic events, such as assassinations, school shootings, crime rampages, and murder-suicides, are the result of such programming? We know that a person can indeed successfully implant an idea or thought in the mind of someone under hypnotic trance or induction. We also know that people can successfully lose weight, stop smoking, end bad habits, or not feel pain during medical procedures because of the suggestive nature of hypnosis and the altered state of mind under induction.

But does this mean that every time something tragic and awful happens in the world, it was the result of a person being programmed by sinister forces adept at mind control? Columbine, Sandy Hook, the Aurora movie theater, the alleged suicides of whistle-blowers, assassinations of presidents and political figures—could the shooters be under some mind programming designed to create specific collective social reactions and behaviors? Psychiatrist Colin Ross, MD, suggests in his many books that cults and various government and military projects use mind control and trauma to split and dissociate people, who can then be manipulated to do things they would not normally do, and act out the desires of the programmers, including murder and mass slaughter.

Conspiracy theorists point to the often-bizarre behavior of the shooters and assassins, including their own statements to the police, their actions in court, and their often-blank stares and strange appearances.

Let's take the Sandy Hook (Connecticut) school shootings as an example.

On December 14, 2012, a young man named Adam Lanza fatally shot his mother, then went to Sandy Hook Elementary School in Newton, Connecticut, and killed 20 students and six staff members before taking his own life. As more about Lanza was revealed by the media, we learned that he was 20 years old, and had a history of some mental disorders, including sensory processing disorder as a child, Asperger's syndrome as a teen, obsessive compulsive disorder, and depression. He was taking Celexa, an anti-depressant, but had stopped taking it, and his father, Peter Lanza, suggested his son may have been suffering from schizophrenia. He allegedly put black tape over his windows, refused to allow anyone into his room, communicated with his mother in later years only via email, was estranged from his brother and father before the shootings, was obsessed with mass shootings, and left a diatribe about women on his computer before he died. His mother, Nancy, had firearms in the house.

Mental illness plus firearm availability equals bad news.

But was he under mind control? There is absolutely no proof he was, and there is absolutely no proof he wasn't. Some conspiracy theorists suggest that his mass shooting, along with others that have made headline news as of late, are all evidence of mind control programming being activated to create "false flags" or trauma events that galvanize or mobilize certain segments of the population, playing into the hands of government agendas and motives. These subjects are nothing but unwitting guinea pigs of an agenda that could include creating fear and divisiveness among the populace, sending "false conspiracies" and disinformation viral over the Internet, YouTube, and social networking, splitting people along party lines, creating religious bigotry, and driving gun sales higher or lower, depending on your point of view. These shooters and assassins may be nothing more than tools by which we, the people, are being manipulated and behaviorally modified.

Or they could just be nut-jobs with guns.

The bummer is, most of these shooters and assassins end up dead, unavailable to be examined under the spotlight of truth. The ones who live end up in prisons or mental institutions, stigmatized forever by their actions, to the point where even if they were patsies in someone else's sick game, no one would believe them except for a fringe segment of society that is equally stigmatized as nut-jobs.

A more intriguing case presents itself with James Holmes, the 24-year-old shooter who killed 12 people and injured 70 others in the Aurora, Colorado, movie theater rampage of July 20, 2012.

Holmes was wearing protective gear, including a gas mask and load-bearing vest, and armed to the teeth when he went into a theater showing a midnight screening of *The Dark Knight Rises* and set off tear gas grenades, then shot up the audience with various firearms, including a

The Century 16 theater in Aurora, Colorado, where the 2012 shooting took place. Image © Algr, made available under the terms of GNU Free Documentation License.

Aurora, Colorado Shooting
7/20/2012

CENTURY

James Holmes
Born: 12/13/1987

© 2014 Robert Preston

A painting of James Holmes from the "Lone Nut Series" by artist Robert Preston (www.robertprestonart.com). Image © Robert Preston. Used with permission.

rifle, a tactical shotgun, and a Glock 22 handgun. Holmes was apprehended later behind the theater and offered no resistance to arrest. His hair was allegedly dyed red and he called himself "the Joker," a look we would all see later in court in Centennial, Colorado. Apparently, he acted alone and had booby-trapped his apartment. The world watched in horror as the events occurred over every news media outlet, and soon the conspiracy theories began.

According to Wayne Madsen, writing for *Blacklisted News*, Holmes was a recipient of a National Institute of Health Neuroscience Training Grant at the University of Colorado's Anschutz Medical Campus in Denver. He graduated with a bachelor of science degree in neuroscience from the University of California, Riverside. Allegedly, before the massacre, Holmes lectured at the Anschutz campus about the "Biological Basis of Psychiatric and Neurological Disorders." The campus buildings were evacuated after Holmes was in custody for the shootings. Anschutz is a de-commissioned site of the U.S. Army's Fitzsimons Army Medical Center and named after Phillip Anschutz, a Christian fundamentalist oil and railroad tycoon, and owner of *The Examiner* and *Weekly Standard*. Holmes, at the age of 18, was a research intern at the SALK Institute in La Jolla, California. The SALK Institute had previously been involved in research for DARPA, the Defense Advance Research Projects Agency, and a number of universities researching ways to prevent fatigue in combat troops using an anti-oxidant flavinol found in dark chocolate. The MARS candy company was also involved.

This research program was a part of DARPA's "Peak Soldier Performance Program" to create brain-machine interfaces for battlefield use, as Madsen's article states. Note that James Holmes's father, Dr. Robert Holmes, was also deeply involved in work involving neural networking and cortronic neural networks that allow a machine to literally interpret stimuli and think like a human. Dr. Robert Holmes, apparently, had even more links to research in neurobiology and defense and government agencies.

But are these links to the defense industry indicative of Holmes being under some kind of sinister influence? Is his own work with the brain and neuroscience a telling indicator that he was somehow triggered to shoot up a movie theater? Are these links suspicious and unusual, or simply "six degrees of separation" and links that we might be able to find connected to anyone if we look deep enough?

Back to Adam Lanza, the Sandy Hook shooter. These tragic events are often suggested to be "false flag" orchestrated events to create a particular behavioral response via the media from the populace, whether that is a push for gun control, or a diversion from another situation the governing bodies don't want attention on. Is the increase of these mass shooting incidents a sign of something bigger, or just a sign of the media covering more of them when they do occur? Lanza was no stranger to the conspiracy theory mill, as his father, Peter Lanza, was a vice president with GE Energy Financial Services. According to the conspiracy theory, Peter Lanza had inside information about the LIBOR scandal, a series of fraudulent actions connected to the LIBOR (London Interbank Offered Rate), an average interest rate calculated through submissions of interest rates by major banks in London. The scandal involved a number of banks falsely inflating or deflating their rates so as to profit from trades, or to give the impression that they were more creditworthy than they were. Peter Lanza was supposed to testify before the Senate Banking Committee, but no such hearings were scheduled. Peter Lanza did go on to tell *The New Yorker*: "With hindsight, I know Adam would have killed me in a heartbeat, if he'd had the chance. I don't question that for a minute. The reason he shot Nancy four times was one for each of us: one for Nancy; one for him; one for [his brother] Ryan; one for me." Were the alleged sins of the father somehow responsible for the son's strange behavior? It's a very big reach to imply so, but the conspiracy lives on.

Mind Control of the Future

In an article for *Activist Post* titled "7 Future Methods of Mind Control," Nicholas West explored some of the possible ways we might be manipulated in the future, by a small and elite group of people, most likely using the technology of tomorrow to coerce, control and contain.

West writes, "The mind control of the future goes straight into direct programming of the digital mind." The seven methods West warns us about are:

1. **Surveillance and gadgets:** West sees both surveillance and the obsession with gadgetry a means by which of controlling the masses, pointing to television and video games as having massive impact on how we view our world. He points to the Internet, computers, phones, tablets, and more as the tools of direct manipulation of our lives. Mind/computer interfacing is already happening now.

2. **Mind-controlled robots and drones:** The merging of man and machine, as evident by brain mapping research. Are there possibly thought-controlled drones in our future?

3. **Magnetic manipulation:** See Chapter 8 for the many means by which our environment is effecting and influencing our thoughts, actions, and behaviors.

4. **Implants and ingestibles:** Will we be controlled via implants and chips that enter the human body through our food, medicines, and other means?

5. **Genetic and neuro-engineering:** A quote by MIT neuro-engineer Ed Boyden sums it up: "If we take seriously the idea that our minds are implemented in the circuits of our brains, then it becomes a top priority to understand how to engineer brains for the better." Maybe also for the worse?

6. **Neuroscience:** The human brain is the final frontier—and controlling it is the Holy Grail of research. Unfortunately, this can be used for evil as well as good.

7. **Direct upload/hack:** Brain hacking is no longer the stuff of science fiction novels, as we become the software-based humans that Ray Kurzweil, author of *The Singularity Is Near* and current director of engineering at Google, warned us about. "Humans will develop the means to instantly create new portions of ourselves, either biological or nonbiological," Kurzweil writes in *The Singularity Is Near.*

Remote "Control"

Imagine a huge and raging bull charging at you, full force, ready to mow you down until you press a button on a small radio transmitter...and stop the bull in its tracks? Well, it has already been achieved, thanks to Dr. Jose M.R. Delgado, a scientist at Yale University's School of Medicine. In 2013, Delgado conducted just such an experiment in Cordova, Spain, proving that a bull could be remote-controlled. Delgado placed electrodes into the bull's brain that later reacted to remote-controlled electrical stimulation, literally changing the bull's behaviors and actions.

Delgado had been working on this experiment in remote-controlled modified behavior for more than 15 years and finally developed the technology that led Delgado to believe science had reached a turning point. He told the New York Times *in a July 2014 article (titled "'Matador' with a Radio Stops Wired Bull Modified Behaviour in Animals the Subject of Brain Study") that "Functions traditionally related to the psyche, such as friendliness, pleasure or verbal expression, can be induced, modified and inhibited by direct stimulation of the brain." Although scientists have been manipulating the brain with electrical stimulation since the 19th century, this brave new research suggests that we might one day be controlled via direct stimulation. This research has not been confined to animals, as Delgado himself has done experiments on human beings, primarily during the treatment of types of epilepsy, where stimulation of the brain's regions have produced anxiety, friendliness, and even increased verbalization in patients.*

The question that must be asked, though, remains: Who will control the remotes?

Whatever our future holds, we will no doubt be faced with constant manipulation of our own "final frontier" as the flow of information increases and technology threatens to evolve at a faster rate than we can keep up with.

Will we lose control?

5

THE CULT CONNECTION:
THE USE OF MIND CONTROL IN CULTS

Cult recruiting methods based on dosing victims with the brain chemicals released during capture bonding would make cults even more of a problem than they are now.
—Keith Henson

What you need to believe in is what you can see.... If you see me as your friend, I'll be your friend. If you see me as your father, I'll be your father, for those of you that don't have a father. If you see me as your savior, I'll be your savior. If you see me as your God, I'll be your God.
—Jim Jones of Peoples Temple

On the web the thinking of cults can spread very rapidly and suddenly a cult which was 12 people who had some deep personal issues suddenly find a formula which is very believable.
—Tim Berners-Lee

JONES: *Please. For God's sake, let's get on with it. We've lived—we've lived as no other people lived and loved. We've had as much of this world as you're gonna get. Let's just be done with it. Let's be done with the agony of it. (Applause.) It's far, far harder to have to walk through every day, die slowly—and from the time you're a child 'til the time you get gray, you're dying. Dishonest, and I'm sure that they'll—they'll pay for it. They'll pay for it. This is a revolutionary suicide. This is not a self-destructive suicide. So they'll pay for this. They brought this upon us. And they'll pay for that. I leave that destiny to them. (Voices.) Who wants to go with their child has a right to go with their child. I think it's humane. I want to go—I want to see you go, though. They can take me and do what they want—whatever they want to do. I want to see you go. I don't want to see you go* *through this hell no more. No more. No more. No more. We're trying. If everybody will relax. The best thing you do to relax, and you will have no problem. You'll have no problem with this thing if you just relax.*

This excerpt is from the "Suicide Tape" transcript of the final speech cult leader of the People's Temple, James Warren "Jim" Jones gave before his followers on November 18, 1978. Deep in the jungles of Guyana, Jones persuaded more than 900 of his devoted followers to end their lives, and the lives of their small children, in what would become the largest mass suicide in history. Though the People's Temple began in 1955 with the positive goals of family-building and gardening, bringing people together to work for the poor and welcome all into its society, it morphed over the next two decades into a religious cult run by a man who cast a spell on those who knew him, and those who had the terrible misfortune to turn their lives and their souls over to him.

Using a combination of rhetoric and justification for the earlier murders of Congressman Leo Ryan and a reporting crew from NBC, who had been gunned down trying to leave Guyana after investigating the cult for human rights violations, Jones employed a feeling of righteousness and loyalty when he asked his followers who remained at the compound with him to die with dignity. These followers had already given their money, their time, and their energy to this man, who called himself a prophet in that same final speech. Now he wanted them to give him their lives as a show of loyalty and to stand united against the outsiders who sought to destroy the community they had built in the jungle.

And those followers—more than 900 of them—ended their lives for their leader, a man who was clearly crazed with power and narcissistic self-aggrandization. A man who thought nothing of asking parents to murder their own children, calling it "an act of revolutionary suicide protesting the conditions of an inhumane world."

Yet what could be more inhumane than asking people to end the lives of their children? You and I can ask such a common-sense question, but to those held captive in a cult, either physically, emotionally, or both, there is no such question. There is no such common sense, for the mind of a cult member has been absconded—emptied and reprogrammed by a leader or leaders bent on imposing their own beliefs and will onto those willing enough to take it.

> **JONES:** *I, with respect, die with a degree of dignity. Lay down your life with dignity. Don't lay down with tears and agony. There's nothing to death. It's like Mac said, it's just stepping over to another plane. Don't be this way. Stop this hysterics. This is not the way for people who are Socialists or Communists to die. No way for us to die. We must die with some dignity. We must die with some dignity. We will have no choice. Now we have some choice. Do you think they're gonna allow this to be done—allow us to get by with this? You must be insane. Look children, it's just something to put you to rest. Oh, God. (Children crying.)*
>
> *Mother, Mother, Mother, Mother, Mother, please. Mother, please, please, please. Don't—don't do this. Don't do this. Lay down your life with your child. But don't do this.*
>
> **WOMAN 14:** *We're doing all of this for you.*
>
> **JONES:** *Free at last. Keep—keep your emotions down. Keep your emotions down. Children, it will not hurt. If you'd be—if you'll be quiet. If you'll be quiet. (Music and crying.) It's never been done before, you say. It's been done by every tribe in history. Every tribe facing annihilation. All the Indians of the Amazon are doing it right now. They refuse to bring any babies into the world. They kill every child that comes into the world. Because they don't want to live in this kind of a world. So be patient. Be patient. Death is—I tell you, I don't care how many screams you hear. I don't care how many anguished cries. Death is a million times preferable to ten more days of this life. If you knew what was ahead of you—if you knew what was ahead of you, you'd be glad to be stepping over tonight.*

As you read the above final words of Jones's "revolutionary suicide" call to action, you most likely feel sick to your stomach at the thought of anyone being so weak and so ignorant as to join a cult. But surprisingly, intelligence has little to do with who ends up drinking poison or eating

Jell-O tainted with cyanide. Cult leaders know that the best minds to control are those attached to people with great empathy, compassion, and a desire to be important and purposeful, which is why, like Jones did, cults tend to isolate their members away from society. It's far easier to tell your members how special they are, to play upon their empathy and compassion, and to take their money and their time, even their sexual favors, without the prying eyes of the outside to bring people back to reality.

Cult of Control

Cults are insidious, pervasive, sick, and dangerous—yet many people belong to cults without even knowing it. The definition of a cult is, quite simply, according to *Merriam-Webster Dictionary*, "a small religious group that is not part of a larger and more accepted religion and that has beliefs regarded by many people as extreme or dangerous." Dictionary. com gets a little more specific, citing a cult as:

Noun

1. a particular system of religious worship, especially with reference to its rites and ceremonies.
2. an instance of great veneration of a person, ideal, or thing, especially as manifested by a body of admirers: the physical fitness cult.
3. the object of such devotion.
4. a group or sect bound together by veneration of the same thing, person, ideal, etc.
5. sociology. A group having a sacred ideology and a set of rites centering around their sacred symbols.
6. a religion or sect considered to be false, unorthodox, or extremist, with members often living outside of conventional society under the direction of a charismatic leader.
7. the members of such a religion or sect.

So, a cult doesn't have to be a religious in nature, but any group that reveres and worships a person or object. Organized religion falls into the definition of a cult. It is indeed in all its forms all about the worship and veneration of a particular leader, and its devoted adherents follow rites and rituals. A cult can even be a group of people who worship turtles.

But what makes these groups so dangerous is how they operate—how they find, recruit, and, more importantly, control their followers. Those tactics involve methods of mind control and behavior modification designed to keep members in line and under the thumb of the leadership. Those who defect often do so at great risk, not just physically, but psychologically, suffering from PTSD, and needing to be "deprogrammed" from the invasive methods employed to keep them obedient and subservient.

As with Jim Jones, most cult leaders are magnetic, charismatic people with the gift of persuasion. That gift is manifested through language and rhetoric designed to lure in people who feel lost, alone, unneeded, left out, cast aside, and different from the normal segments of society. Cult leaders prey upon the kind, the giving, the caring, the sympathetic, and the lost, just as a narcissist or psychopath does. Intelligence has nothing to do with it, for many a smart man or woman has fallen prey to the enigmatic lure of a cult that made him or her feel special, needed, purposeful, and empowered.

Ideological vs. Personal

There are two kinds of cults. One revolves around the charisma of a particular leader, who gathers his or her followers like disciples and lays down the rules and regulations the members will adhere to, or be cast out for disobeying. Charismatic cult leaders like David Koresh, Charles Manson, Jim Jones, and others are the main draw. Yes, they promote a certain ideology and doctrine, but their ability to draw and persuade is the glue that holds the cult in place. If they die, or have a change of heart, the cult will probably fall apart after time. Hitler could be said to be a cult leader, as could religious leaders of every ilk, the good, bad, and ugly. Using rhetoric, body language, and personal magnetism is a must for getting others to turn over their life to you and your mission, and the most prolific cult leaders know this inherently.

Ideological cults focus more on a set of shared beliefs. The Ku Klux Klan can be classified as a cult that centers on white racial supremacy. The leadership is not worshipped; the beliefs are. Recruits are expected to adopt those beliefs and behave accordingly, even to the point of committing crimes and murder. Racially motivated and religiously motivated cults often are ideological in nature. There may be a leader of a particular group or organization, but the power of that individual is not paramount to the continuation of the cult if he or she dies. Political and "self-help" cults are more focused on pushing a particular mind-set, such as liberalism or conservatism, or in the case of new age cults, a way of utilizing certain tools and techniques to better one's life, even if in some case you are turning over your pocketbook contents to do so.

Remember Patty Hearst, heir to the Hearst newspaper fortune, who was kidnapped by an organization called the Symbionese Liberation Army (SLA) in 1974? Hearst, in a classic example of Stockholm Syndrome, later became one with her captors, even supporting and committing crimes in the name of "their" revolution, despite having been abused, tortured, and brainwashed in their presence. Hearst would later tell talk show giant Larry King that she had no idea at the time she was being brainwashed.

Hearst, who documented her experiences in her 1983 book, *Every Secret Thing*, was blindfolded, confined to a dark closet, tortured and raped, and subjected to a program of "indoctrination and re-education," as well as humiliation for her wealthy upbringing that served to shame her and alienate her from her family of origin. Donald "Cinque" De-Freeze, the SLA leader, interrogated her constantly, told her over and over again how "Amerikkka" was a racist and evil society, and told her she was a "bourgeoisie bitch" and her father a "pig" of the "corporate fascist state." Intertwined with this indoctrination were tidbits of kindness, such as offerings of food or liquids, and then the torment would begin again in classic capture bonding style.

She told Larry King, "Most of the time I was with them, my mind was going through doing exactly what I was supposed to do...I had no freewill."

Not only did Hearst become dependent on her captors for survival, but for some promise of emotional balance as well, even if it was only in the form of crumbs of positive reinforcement. Eventually, she adopted their worldview, and became one of their freedom fighters, robbing banks alongside them dressed in black. She had fallen prey to the rhetoric of leaders who had a mission, a mission she even accepted as her own after brutal behavioral alteration methods forced her to give up her own worldview for that of a group she had never heard of before her own life changed at their hands.

Most cults include both personal and ideological forces, but a careful look will expose one as being more critical to the success of the cult than another. Personal cults tend to be more sensationalized in the media, because who isn't fascinated by the thought that one person can attract a huge following, and make that following do his or her bidding?

Scientology

Scientology is a perfect example of a cult that focuses both on an individual leader and an ideology or structure of beliefs. Scientology originated with the teachings of a science fiction author turned self-help guru L. Ron Hubbard in the early 1950s. Based upon Hubbard's earlier system called "Dianetics," which can best be described as a system to control the mind by doing away with mental blocks and fears, and the book *Dianetics: The Modern Science of Mental Health* published in 1950, Hubbard went on to create the Church of Scientology and incorporated it as a religion in Camden, New Jersey. Now a global phenomenon, Scientology claims to be a bridge between Eastern and Western philosophies that "constitutes Man's first real application of scientific methodology to spiritual questions," according to its Website.

But many critics leveled the word *cult* at the organization after allegations emerged of brainwashing techniques and psychological abuse, even fraud of its own members. Some of those members include prominent actors and celebrities who firmly believe in the counseling technique known as "auditing," or consciously recalling fearful and traumatic events until they can be cleared from the mind and consciousness, and appear to be quite successful. Yet others who leave the organization whistle-blow about strong-arm tactics against members, especially those who show a desire to leave. This is not the behavior of a "church," but of a "cult," and yet many such pseudo-religious organizations walk the fine line.

In a September 2014 story for the *UK Daily Mail Online*, reporter Laura Collins interviewed Karen de la Carriere, who was a 35-year high-ranking member (she was the wife of the president) of Scientology before she decided to jump ship. But first she questioned what she saw as misbehavior on the part of the notoriously secretive organization, and was met with such brutal punishments as being forced to run around a pole for 12 hours a day for three months, or being imprisoned in a place called "The Hole," where her job was to literally chip paint off a metal pole for days on end while her young son was being kept from her and she was not allowed to shower or change clothes. Her own son later turned on her when she left the organization. He died of pneumonia and de la Carriere believed it was the organization's refusal to allow him any healthcare other than its own healing method that killed him so young.

What stands out in her story is the fraud she began witnessing, involving breaches of power and taking funds from members, and how any kind of questioning of those ethic breaches led to severe punishment. Also, upon finally exiting the organization, the absolute quest to destroy her is common among cults, especially those of a religious bent that cannot afford its remaining members to begin asking questions as well. De la Carriere stated that, "Scientology is like a tsunami of destruction. It launches at you and when it retreats it leaves behind broken lives, damaged people, bankrupt people, people who thought they were buying a dream, but were sold a monster." Lucky for her she got out, unlike the followers of Peoples Temple leader Jim Jones, who went down with the monster.

Another chilling story of a Scientology member came from the *Tampa Bay Times*. In a March 2014 article titled "Scientology Clergy Force a Mother to Choose: Son or Daughter," part of an ongoing study called "Inside Scientology," reporter Joe Childs interviewed Sara Goldberg, a former church member who was punished severely by the leadership for refusing to "disconnect" from her son, Nick, who had been raised in Scientology but later formed an alliance with church whistleblowers. Goldberg's daughter remained loyal to the church, and Goldberg was forced to shun her son or leave the church, and her daughter, behind.

Reporter Joe Childs states that Scientology offers grave consequences to any member who refuses to disconnect from rogue family members or non-Scientologists, which the church refers to as "SP," or suppressive persons: "Scientologists tend to socialize within their tight-knit community, work for employers who are Scientologists and patronize members' businesses. Disconnection can mean not only near-total social isolation, but also financial hazard. Also threatened is salvation. Scientologists believe that auditing is the path to eternity. SPs and potential trouble sources are banned from church services."

But this kind of shunning is not exclusive to Scientology.

7 Signs and Bethany's Story

In a chilling article titled "The Seven Signs You're in a Cult," written by Boze Herrington for the *Atlantic Online*, we get an inside glimpse into the ways a mind can succumb to the thoughts and beliefs of another. Herrington tells his own story as a former member of a religious prayer group affiliated with IHOP, the International House of Prayer, that he realized all too late was a cult—too late because the cult was responsible for the suicide of Herrington's best friend, Bethany Leidlein, a fellow student he had spent time with in a prayer group on campus at Southwestern University in Texas. The group drew upon the teachings of IHOP, and the IHOP founder had actually created a list of ways to determine the difference between a religious organization and a cult:

1. Opposes critical thinking.
2. Isolates members and penalizes them for leaving.
3. Emphasizes special doctrine outside of scripture.
4. Seeks inappropriate loyalty to their leaders.
5. Dishonors the family unit.
6. Crosses biblical boundaries of behavior (i.e., sexual purity, personal ownership).
7. Separate from the Church.

Yet as time went on, the prayer group, under the direction and leadership of a classmate named Tyler Deaton, began to look just like the above: a cult, albeit a cult founded upon evangelical Christian beliefs taken to the extreme. Following Tyler Deaton, who Herrington claims intended to launch a "spiritual revolution" on campus, was thrilling for the author of the article at first. He felt he belonged to something extraordinary: "I was lonely and bored, and I wanted to experience something extraordinary before I left school: a mystery to be solved, a battle to fight, a romantic quest, like the heroes in the stories I had read." Deaton's cause served just such an adventure: "I had always imagined my life in terms of a story, and now Tyler was offering me the chance to be a part of one."

Unfortunately, this story ended with the suicide of Bethany, who was a member of this tight-knit prayer group. Herrington had been kicked out of the group after being accused of having a wicked heart, among other things, and was isolated as the other members stopped speaking to him (another mind control punishment tactic). Herrington was being shunned, a classic method of behavioral modification. But Herrington returned to the group, although upon his return, he began to see the clear signs of abuse and cult behavior on behalf of the leadership. He stated that even the slightest innocent gesture was looked upon as a sign of demonic influence by the group, whose leader Tyler Deaton was making bolder claims of God speaking to him and directing him.

Bethany, meanwhile, was drawn to Tyler and eventually they became engaged. Herrington was kicked out of the prayer community again, shunned from the community and his best friend, Bethany. Then he heard of her death, and a following investigation that showed a member of the group named Micah had murdered Bethany at Tyler Deaton's request.

It was no suicide.

For the dead at Jonestown, perhaps it was not suicide either, but murder at the hands of a master manipulator using language, emotion, claims of divinity, and a host of other tactics to cast a spell on a crowd and make them willing to do his bidding. As with Tyler Deaton, guilty of one murder, or Jones, guilty of inciting a mass murder, the ability to charm and beguile is paramount. Once charmed, emotional and physical abuse, and even sexual abuse, is often possible, even acceptable, among members who are so devoted to a higher cause and a leader they believe has been touched by God.

In the previous chapter, we discussed the three powerful impacts of rhetoric:

- **Logos:** Using logical arguments such as induction and deduction.
- **Pathos:** Creating an emotional reaction in the audience.
- **Ethos:** Projecting a trustworthy, charismatic authority image.

The most effective cult leaders do all three, but they also employ the use of *solus*, or isolating their followers, either by taking them out into the middle of the jungle, or by isolating individuals who disobey the rules and need to be punished. This applies to churches, not just cults, as stories abound of people who have been shunned and outcast after attempting to leave an evangelical or fundamentalist church.

Many former cult members also report ongoing uses of emotional and physical abuse as methods of breaking down individual will and achieving compliance and obedience, but a cult doesn't always have to go to those extremes. Sometimes, all it takes is talking to your members in a way that makes them feel special, and makes them feel even *more* special for following you. Add to that key factors on behalf of both the members and the leaders, and you have the perfect brew for a perfect storm.

In "Obey Your Father: Jim Jones' Rhetoric of Deadly Persuasion," author Jacob Neighbors sums up this perfect storm, perfectly, stating: "The strength of a movement is determined neither by the ideology it reflects nor by the opposition it faces; it is determined by the might of those who follow it." True that no cult can exist without members willing to put their money and their lives on the line for the leader's ideology. Neighbors continues:

> The concept of gaining power through an inflated following is the source of Jones' insatiable thirst for new recruits. The more people Jones could seduce, the more power and influence he was able to flex. These influences are ultimately what shaped Jones' never-ending quest to attract and sustain a robust following, and Jones, through manipulation of his own *ethos* and his following's *solus*, was a leader who had tremendous skill in doing just that.

By isolating followers, a leader can more easily use the art of rhetorical persuasion to convince them of why they are following. Jones also played upon his "divinity" by claiming to heal and to be a servant of God, a claim used by many a cult leader in a world where millions of people long to be healed, to be saved, to be led—even if they are led to their own deaths.

One final factor Neighbors points out drives home the ability of a true charismatic to overcome objections and rationalizations by his or her members. That Jones took his followers into a very isolated setting, and then imposed upon them a set of values that separated them all from the evil outside world, was a masterful ploy at creating his own elevation, with the ethos of his rhetoric, and his followers' diminished power, through solus or solitude and isolation, by keeping them from the potential influences of the outsiders who might shake them out of their reverie and bring them back to reality. No doubt many cult followers develop capture bonding or Stockholm Syndrome, even when they suspect on a deeper level they are being abused. They come to revere and adore the leader(s) who took them in, gave them a sense of belonging, and cared for them when no one else did. That they might also have had to give up their homes, families, money, bodies, and will becomes secondary to the devotion they feel to their leader, until some event wakes them up, or some outside source pokes a hole in their bubble of illusion.

Group Dynamics

Although cults seem to operate in isolation, they exist upon the dynamics of a group working together for a common goal. There are actually certain behaviors evident in a group of people involving role identification, decision-making, cohesion, and communication that become almost like rituals depending on the group, or, in this case, the cult. As a member, an individual often gives up his or her core identity to become a part of the group dynamic, and goes with the direction of the group, even against his or her own values and integrity.

To go against the group means not only harsh punishment from the leadership, but from fellow group members who see any kind of out-of-the-box thinking or behavior as a potential fatal flaw in the delicate structure they have bought into. Someone who goes against the group might be someone who has figured out the truth, or seen the reality behind the more sinister purposes of the group itself, and members will shun and punish—even harm—that person to keep the group identity intact. Conflicts are dealt with swiftly and often involve threats to both conflicted parties. It's all about keeping the peace, or the illusion, at all costs.

In 1972, social psychologist Irving Janis, author of *Victims of Group-think*, coined the term *groupthink* to identify what happens when a group makes decisions because of group pressures and expectations, often which lead to a deterioration of "mental efficiency, reality testing, and moral judgment." Groupthink ignores alternatives and often promotes irrational actions that dehumanize other groups. "A group is especially vulnerable to groupthink when its members are similar in background, when the group is insulated from outside opinions, and when there are no clear rules for decision making," Janis writes.

According to Janis, there are eight symptoms of groupthink:

1. **Illusion of invulnerability:** Creates excessive optimism that encourages taking extreme risks.

2. **Collective rationalization:** Members discount warnings and do not reconsider their assumptions.

3. **Belief in inherent morality:** Members believe in the rightness of their cause and therefore ignore the ethical or moral consequences of their decisions.

4. **Stereotyped views of out-groups:** Negative views of "enemy" make effective responses to conflict seem unnecessary.

5. **Direct pressure on dissenters:** Members are under pressure not to express arguments against any of the group's views.

6. **Self-censorship:** Doubts and deviations from the perceived group consensus are not expressed.

7. **Illusion of unanimity:** The majority view and judgments are assumed to be unanimous.

8. **Self-appointed "mindguards":** Members protect the group and the leader from information that is problematic or contradictory to the group's cohesiveness, view, and/or decisions.

Cults employ groupthink, just as religions and political groups do. In fact, get a group of like-minded people together under any circumstance and this sometimes dangerous "mob mentality" is likely to happen.

For someone trapped in a cult, or even there willingly, the desire to "go along to get alone" overcomes the desire to be an individual with a unique viewpoint and expression of the world.

Aliens and Gates of Heaven

The UFO Millennial cult Heaven's Gate made headlines in March 1997 when police in Rancho Santa Fe, California, discovered the bodies of 39 members of a cult run by a man and a woman named Marshall Applewhite and Bonnie Nettles, aka "Bo and Peep" and "Do and Ti." The Heaven's Gate cult was basically a group of people who believed that they would join an alien mother ship en route to the Comet Hale-Bopp if they took their lives en masse. They did so, as an "evacuation of this Earth," as their leader Marshall Applewhite put it, by taking Phenobarbital mixed into apple sauce and washed down with vodka, then putting plastic bags over their heads to asphyxiate themselves.

The dead were found lying nice and neat in the bunk beds of the 9,200-square-foot mansion they lived in, their faces and upper bodies covered in purple cloth. Each one carried in their pocket an "interplanetary toll" of five dollars and three quarters. Interestingly, they were all dressed in brand-new Nikes, and black sweat pants and shirts, and all wore armbands reading "Heaven's Gate Away Team."

To someone who is not aware of this event, it may almost sound comical—that a group of people between the ages of 26 and 72 could believe such things to the point of killing themselves for an interplanetary soul rendezvous. But 39 people did believe this (and two more who were not present killed themselves in the same manner at a later date)—so strongly that they killed themselves, causing untold shock and grief for the people they left behind, who could not understand the charisma and magnetism of Applewhite and Nettles (who died in 1985) and the desire to be a part of something far grander than life on an earth they saw as about to be "recycled."

These "end times" beliefs are prominent in many cults, even causing people to buy into what, to us outsiders, might seem cartoonish and outlandish. The Heaven's Gate members were not stupid; in fact, they were considered very computer and tech savvy, and to those who live in the area, as co-author Marie does, they were described as kind and "normal" by members of the community who had the fortune to interact with them before their mass exodus.

But something made them all take their lives. Something made them believe in the tales told by two people—tales involving aliens and a comet to salvation and life on other planets. Applewhite, their fearless leader, led a pretty normal life until he met Nettles in 1972. They began discussing mysticism and metaphysical concepts, and somehow became certain they were chosen as divine messengers, a belief that expanded as they traveled about the Pacific Northwest, collecting followers. After Nettles died, Applewhite learned of the pending arrival of Comet Hale-Bopp and began to plan for a journey off of planet Earth with his followers. Though there was only one survivor of the mass suicide, there is not a lot of information on the tactics Applewhite used to persuade intelligent people to leave the planet for a comet ride, but commentators suggest he utilized charisma, rhetoric, and the belief that he was a divine figure sent to lead his flock. He also employed the use of solus, or isolation, by keeping his flock somewhat nomadic, so they could not put down roots, and combining a belief in extraterrestrials with the ideology of the Book of Revelations to develop a unique end of the world insight that only he and his followers shared.

Strict obedience was demanded by followers, and there was little contact permitted with outside sources, and even security against infiltration from hostile parties. Yet Applewhite was not dictatorial. Instead he was said to be more of a father figure, one his members were encouraged to go to for guidance and moral direction. Members did live secretive lives at various locations, usually campgrounds, and were put through a sort of boot camp to prepare them for the next level of existence to come. Members were, however, allowed to visit with family on certain special days, like Mother's Day. This combination of both control and freedom was a heady mix to those who resonated with the alien concepts the group embraced.

Coercive cult mind control tactics need not be bold and direct and even domineering. Kill 'em with kindness, although "keep an eye on them and their money" does the trick just as well. Some cults even allow freedom of expression, as long as that expression stays within a certain predetermined range of acceptable expressions laid down by the leadership! Yet, add in some subtle things like intimidation, a forced environment, and an emphasis on an "us versus them" mentality, and members fall deep into a trap they had no idea they had even fallen into in the first place.

According to Margaret Singer, famed anti-cultist and psychologist, the best way to control another person's behavior is through guilt and fear. She identifies several types of guilt that are coercive, including identity guilt, family guilt, guilt over past deeds, and guilt over thoughts and feelings. Guilt and shame are powerful tools of religious cults that play upon a person's sins and promise forgiveness and salvation. Throw in fear of being punished, by both the cult leadership and God, and control is complete. Tell the members they will be shunned if they leave, or worse, and control is guaranteed to last.

But often this is done in subtle ways. Dr. Singer suggests that coercion in small steps serves to assure that the victim, in this case the cult member, does not notice the changes occurring in themselves or his or her surroundings until it is too late, if ever. And when applied in a group dynamic, the victim is even more inclined to go along with those subtle changes, especially because everyone else is. Eventually, the behavior of the controlled person creates a strong sense of dependency, something key to keeping cult members in line and obedient. The controlled person forgets what it was ever like to be an autonomous person, acting alone and of his or her own volition. Because cult leaders use a person's basic desire to respect authority and desire a peaceful communal existence, they succeed at being able to exploit the person financially, emotionally, and even sexually without much, if any, resistance.

In 1961, American psychiatrist and author Robert J. Lifton, who focused on the psychological implications of war and political violence, wrote in his book *Thought Reform and the Psychology of Totalism* the eight marks of a true "mind control cult:"

1. **Milieu control:** Milieu is French for "surroundings, environment." Cults control the environment of their recruits mainly by isolation and by keeping them from outside sources of news and information that might cause them to have alternative points of view or beliefs from the cult. By keeping members from seeing the news or the Internet, cults create tunnel vision in their members to keep them focused on the cult.

2. **Mystical manipulation:** Religious cults use God as an overlord to force obedience of recruits. If they disobey, God will punish them. If they are good, God will reward them in Heaven. Fasting,

chanting, and sleep deprivation are often used to create an intense mystical quality that makes members believe they are part of a chosen group.

3. **Purity:** Purity of body and mind, and avoidance of all things "evil," including sex (unless it is with the cult leaders; then it is acceptable!).

4. **The Cult of Confession:** Sins must be confessed immediately. Members are to tattle on other members they see committing acts against cult rules. Leaders use the sin of members as a way to feel superior over them.

5. **Sacred science:** The ideology of the cult is sacred and the one true moral vision for the ordering of human existence. Because it is sacred, it is not questioned.

6. **Loaded language:** The prolific use of phrases designed to end controversial discussion or terminate debate. This language terminates thought, as in "the truth." You either accept, or discussion is over. Words are often deified and chosen to induce psychological force.

7. **Doctrine over people:** Doctrine is number one, even over actual human experience. Even common-sense perceptions are altered to fit cult doctrine. Individuals are not anywhere near as important as the cult's ideology.

8. **Dispensing of existence:** It is up to the cult who can exist and who should not. In the final battle between good and evil, the cult decides who survives and who is cast out, including families. This is also a key tenet of a totalistic movement. Think Nazi Germany, where people were put to death for doctrinal shortcomings.

Again, these cult characteristics can also be applied to any organized religion or even political movement.

Preaching Violence

In many cases, cults find a way to include violence and even murder into their repertoire of beliefs. Members go along willingly, even to the extent of killing themselves and family members. In the case of two very enigmatic cult leaders, violence was necessary for furthering the agenda.

Charles Manson and David Koresh come to mind.

On February 28, 1993, a clash between law enforcement officials and a cult-like religious sect called the Branch Davidians took place, resulting in the deaths of 76 people, including 17 children and the leader of the sect, David Koresh, who believed himself to be a prophet. Koresh, who was born Vernon Wayne Howell, before changing his name in 1990, joined the Branch Davidians in 1982 when he moved to Waco, Texas, and soon began claiming himself to be a prophet, even as he was pursuing a musical career. He broke off into a splinter group after a power coup and moved, with two dozen followers, to a camp just outside of Waco, where they set up and lived for two years before resettling in the Mount Carmel Center camp of the former leader of the group.

Koresh, who chose his new name carefully for its associations with David, the biblical king, and the Persian name of Cyrus the Great, Koresh, who was considered a Messiah, began convincing his fellow members of his Messianic visions and that he had been divinely commissioned to lead. But allegations of child sexual abuse, rape, and stockpiling weapons soon put Koresh and followers on a direct track with ATF agents, who raided the camp in 1993 in what amounted to a 51-day siege, which ended on April 19, 1993, with horrific results.

Though Koresh remains a hero to anti-government factions, the behaviors were typical of an apocalyptic cult waiting for the world to end and be saved by their illustrious leader. Koresh used his charisma and claims of divine direction to wield power and influence over his fellow members, especially the both single and married female ones who he allegedly had "spiritual marriages" with. To some, Koresh was an opportunist who couldn't hack it as a musician, and found another way to get the adoration and adulation he craved.

And then there is another "musician" who had no issue at all with violence, even sending his followers out to slaughter at his bidding. Charles Milles Maddox, who later became Charles Milles Manson, began his criminal life at the age of 9 during a chaotic childhood, as a burglar and car thief. He would do prison time on and off, eventually ending up in the McNeil Island Penitentiary in 1960, where he met the infamous Alvin "Creepy" Karpis, a former member of the Ma Barker Gang, who taught Manson how to play guitar. Manson was obsessed with becoming a musician, a motivation that would later lead him to send his followers to kill Terry Melcher, who he believed was going to launch his musical career.

Eventually, Manson hooked up with some of his followers in San Francisco's Haight-Ashbury, calling himself a guru. These were eople who knew of him and his goals, and he settled in California at the Spahn Ranch, north of the San Fernando Valley outside of L.A. There, he began imposing his beliefs in a coming race war and formed a religious philosophy that borrowed from every other religion, including Satanism and Scientology, and even the Beatles song "Helter Skelter," which Manson felt was a prediction of an

2011 mug shot of Charles Manson. Images courtesy of the California Department of Corrections and Rehabilitation.

event to occur in the summer of 1969, when black people would rise up and slaughter white people. It never happened, so Manson turned instead to trying to force black people to rise up and even precipitating the revolution with murderous acts.

Manson's twisted ideology would enable his members, who had become known as "the family," to go to the home he thought belonged to Terry Melcher, who had shunned him earlier in his musical pursuits, and kill him. But when his followers arrived at 10050 Cielo Drive in Los Angeles, Melcher no longer lived there. Instead, four Manson family members brutally slaughtered actress Sharon Tate and her unborn baby, and four other people visiting her while her husband, Roman Polanski, was filming a movie in Europe.

In December 1969, Manson and his followers were arrested, and in January 1970 Manson was convicted of first degree murder and conspiracy to commit murder, and sentenced to death, which was overturned when the California Supreme Court outlawed the death penalty in 1972. Manson is still in jail at Corcoran Prison.

The question to ask here is not how this all happened, but why. The rantings of a man clearly crazy and power-mad somehow moved other people to not only believe him, but to act on his behalf, even to the point of killing innocent human beings in a bloodbath.

Both Koresh and Manson made their members feel like they were chosen, unique—part of a "family"—and both manipulated their members into taking on behaviors that most likely they never would have otherwise. Only a cult of both personality and ideology has this kind of power. They recruit their members with promises of exclusivism, special treatment, and belonging, but soon turn into forces of deception, manipulation, and, eventually, total control of behavior, thought, emotion, and action. These are the most dangerous cults of all.

Deprogramming and Getting Out

Can you get out? If brainwashing and mind control are a pervasive part of being a member of a cult, can just walking away restore life to a balance of normalcy?

People leave a cult when they become aware of the damage it is doing to themselves, their families, and those involved. They leave when they see signs of hypocrisy, fraud, and corruption. They leave when something happens to clear the fog of mind control manipulation. Sometimes they are kicked out for not agreeing to go along with rules and regulations, or for questioning authority and challenging doctrine.

But they, as we've seen with Scientology, don't leave without scars. Often the PTSD of the deception and manipulation, abuse and degradation, fear and intimidation they experienced stays with cult members for years, not to mention the shame, guilt, and financial disaster if they turned over life savings to some shady character with a shadier message. Co-dependency is a huge factor, having become totally dependent on cult leadership for direction and even survival, and once on "the outside," there is a huge sense of loss and confusion.

Psychological harm is common, and often requires the help of a very understanding psychologist or therapist who has some skills in deprogramming the beliefs, behaviors, and doctrines that the former cult member is still haunted by.

Deprogramming got a bad rap in the past, when families would kidnap cult members, isolate them, and then bring in a deprogrammer to wipe their mental slate clean and take out the programming the cult put in, basically. This was common in the 1970s, when a cult member might be forcefully removed from the group by concerned family or friends, and then subjected to intense debriefing courtesy of a trained, and often highly paid, deprogrammer, against his or her will of course. The idea was to counter all of the ideas and values and beliefs imposed during the time under the influence of the cult with new ideas and values and beliefs. Sometimes deprogrammers were former cult members themselves, with an insider understanding of the manipulative tactics the person was dealing with. The problem was some cult members objected to the forceful kidnapping, even going so far as to sue the deprogrammers. Some even returned to the cults they were taken from!

Ted Patrick, one of the pioneers of deprogramming and a controversial figure for his aggressive methods, often brought in psychiatrists and other mental health professionals. Patrick had no formal training and claimed he got into deprogramming when his own son was in a cult. Yet he became known as the "grandfather of deprogramming" when families began hiring him to help them with loved ones trapped in cults. He had many criminal charges against him, including violations of civil rights, abusive methods, and religious rights violations, some resulting in felony convictions. His method, however, included five rather common-sense methods of debriefing:

1. Discredit the cult leader and other authority figures.
2. Present contradicting ideologies and expose hypocrisies.
3. Look for a breaking point when the cult member seems to be emerging from his brainwashed reality and listening to the deprogrammer.
4. Encourage self-expression and allow the member to open up and voice her anger and fear and criticism of the cult.
5. Identification/transference—when the cult member begins to identify with the deprogrammer and oppose the cult leaders/teachings.

Debriefing itself doesn't have to be forceful or violent. It involves asking the cult member to think for themselves in a critical fashion, express individuality, and bring back an emotional connection to the life the member had before cult involvement. It is a type of re-educating of the mind and re-teaching individual and autonomous thinking.

Because some earlier forms of deprogramming were associated with kidnapping and isolating, even more violent methods of debriefing that might include coercion (how does this make the deprogramming any more ethical than the cult?) and cries of civil rights violations, newer methods of dealing with cult members who wish to return to society as normal as possible involve what is called "exit counseling." This is done without force and is not nearly as expensive as paying an alleged deprogrammer. Exit counseling is therapy for both the former cult member and his or her family so that everyone can take part in the member's return to normalcy without judgment. The danger with any kind of cult member counseling lies in not making the person feel as though he is being judged, condemned, ashamed, or guilted, which might cause him to return to the cult!

It is sad that some former cult members will never be normal again, and others can overcome it quite easily; this individual nature of abuse is what makes it difficult to find quality psychological intervention and care. Many therapists just don't have the tools to know how to handle someone who has been abused, deceived, and brainwashed. Perhaps we can be thankful for the advent of the Internet and access to books, forums, and organizations that are devoted to helping cult members get control of their minds, and their lives, again. Discernment with any help goes a long way, as not everything on the Internet is helpful, but former cult members need never feel alone again, and that is one big step toward a return to being an individual with free will and choice.

Cult Stories: 3 Survivors Speak

A Cult Experience
By Pearry Teo

Growing up in a cult was perhaps a very strange experience in my life. Certainly, I did not go about being fearful, nor was I ever placed in a position that would be harmful to me as a child—physically. Throughout growing up, I was never in a situation where my family was poor or hurting for food, but I was certainly denied the luxuries of the outside world. Things like television were banned in my house, I could only hear gospel music, and every single book I read had to be screened by my parents first. Of course, I felt this helped contribute to my creativity once I got older, as being deprived of sensory enjoyment through media, I resorted a lot of my entertainment through my own imagination.

When my mother and father were divorced, it was during the same time the church decided to split up into two as well. They quickly made my parents choose sides and as I grew older, I began to realize that they used God's name in order to make sure my mom and dad did not get back together, because who can deny that they tithe really well? Mind manipulations such as coming to my house and praying over my mom until she cried made me uneasy [so] that one day I decided to chase them out of the house. Since then, they have manipulated my mother's train of thinking to believing I was possessed by the devil and to this day, she still feels embarrassed by my existence because I did not follow this church.

There's nothing wrong with being non-denominational as a church. But it definitely irks me to see them worship some prophet whom they believe to be the last prophet before the second coming of Christ. They seem to worship the man more than God himself. Church go-ers were subjected to lengthy studies of his sermons. We were told never to date outside 'The Word' and consider everybody else evil. Within the church, they have scammed money (out of my father eventually) millions of dollars into properties, producing audiotapes of sermons and the church choir to be distributed freely among church go-ers. Within the church is a complicated system of family boarding to the point they have set up a school behind the church (a non-charter school) where the kids can get their education all year long.

As I grew up, I begin to see a very psychologically unhealthy trend of trying to keep everybody within the family. We only addressed each other as brothers and sisters (but encouraged to marry each other). Of course, how all this has affected me didn't do much the minute I decided that I wanted to have nothing to do with it. They didn't make much effort to stop me. They did send people over to my house to pray and try to get women to take me out on dates to attract me back to the church. Nothing really worked. They gave up within six months and this was it for me.

The truth is, I came out of the place a better person. The amount of things I was denied as a child led to my own unique set of abilities as a human and an artist with a different perspective on life. While I see the good in it, there is definitely no doubt I worry more about the people who follow faith blindly. Christianity is about God, not about trying to create a cult/sect-like scenario for your own ego.

Oh, I forgot to mention: Only men were allowed to preach. Women's roles were to sit down, be quiet, sing songs in church, and breed babies. That's how my mother's mentality is to this day; there is a certain part of me that wish I could change that. But as long as she is happy, I try to keep my opinions to myself.

Breaking Free
By Anonymous

My entire life we moved. We never stayed in anyplace more than two years. My father was always looking to try something new or looking for a different career. I was *always* the new kid and always having to say goodbye to friends. He had been in the military and always just kept moving. I was born in Minneapolis and then as a baby moved to San Antonio.

We moved several times in San Antonio and then my parents took a job working at a Catholic Children's home in San Antonio, Texas. They were live-in foster parents to a home full of abused and neglected children. I lived there with them. I was sent to private Catholic school, and when my parents worked I was taken care of by the nuns. We were there for a couple years and it is where my brother was born. It was during this time that my parents started to attend a local Methodist church and Sunday school group.

The group was led by a man named Lew Schaffer. (This is his real name.) Before long we moved away from the children's home but we began spending more time with the people from this church. One couple became my brother's godparents.

It was just a matter of time before we moved again, this time to another city and away from the group. We lived in El Paso and then [moved] to Florida. Both my parents worked and although my father switched careers a lot, they both did very well for themselves and money was never an issue. During this time, Lew and another man named Ted Platt (along with their wives Sandy and Barbara) had decided to buy property in a town called Azle, Texas, and start their own "mission group." It was several acres with a house and three-car garage. The house was called "the big house" and the garage was turned into a chapel. They started to do "mission work" based on the Bible. They held marriage, women's, and men's seminars, and counseling. The biggest draw of this was that they were taking their mission work international. They sent out newsletters on yellow paper with black and white photos showing the property and photos from China, Germany, and Australia. They asked for people to come and be a part of this—but only if God told them in prayer that you were invited.

It wasn't long before my father was lured into the idea of traveling the world and not having to pay for it. He had majored in world religion in college and already knew a lot. We sold our big house, both our cars, and everything else we had to sell, and off we went. We were moved into a large double-wide trailer on the property and were told my parents could no longer work. We had to live strictly off donations and had to have faith that God would provide. After our savings was gone we ended up living off of my grandparents and food stamps.

Living there wasn't so bad at first. The property was beautiful and there were kids there my age. We had a bumper pool table, a chapel that was always open with a piano, and a kick-ass stereo. Of course "secular" music was frowned upon. The very best thing that happened to me was that I was able to go to middle school then high school at a school [that] had a great football team and went to state. Football in Texas—nothing like it. The town literally shut down for the games. I will always have that in my heart and soul. My other saving grace was that I could sing and was heavily involved in theater and the productions at school, which had me there several nights during the week away from the religion.

It was hard starting school at first, as the rumor was that the people at this ministry were biting the heads off bats and chickens. That's always fun to walk into. Thankfully I also knew who Ozzy was and quickly put that myth to rest. The "ministry" or, as I call it, the cult had two mottos:

1. Jesus Is the Answer
2. Pray about EVERYTHING

I questioned the Bible stories and was told a man *could* live in the belly of a whale, and I had to believe it because I had to have faith. I questioned *everything* and was told I would go to hell if I didn't believe. Those were the only explanations I would get. They expected you to pray about what you ate, wore, and did throughout the entire day. I never did it and was furious when I was asked to. I would lie and say God said to do whatever I wanted to do. God loved the mall apparently. While living there I began to see things that, to this day, have scared me. They believed that the *man* was the head of the household and no one could do anything without permission from that person. Not only did they believe this they lived it. I would ask my mom if I could run to a friend's and she would say, "Let me call your dad and ask him to pray about it and see what God thinks." Seeing my mom do this all the time made me sick!!

She started to say that I couldn't *ask* if I could go.I had to ask if they could *pray* if I could go. My dad didn't even buy it and he would say, "Go if you want." He would even *tell* my mom to make a decision, and she began to feel like she couldn't do anything without his input. It was so hard to see this happening to my mom. I could no longer look up to her or be proud of who she had been. She still loved me but I was angry with her. She had lost a necklace and asked me if I had taken it. (I didn't.) I told her no. She didn't believe me. I said, "You pray, right?" "Yes." "About *everything*, right?" "YES." "And God answers you?" "*Yes.*" "Then ask him if I borrowed or took your necklace." She said, "I did pray and he told me you did." I told her that her God was full of shit and maybe there was no God! I had committed what they called the unforgivable sin. You can kill, rape, and rob, and ask forgiveness and go to heaven, but if you say you don't believe there is a God you go to hell no matter what you do. She lost it and I lost all my religion in that moment.

The heads of the ministry lived in nice houses and were always taking ministry trips to China, San Francisco, Australia, etc. My parents started to get to go on trips as well, to Illinois, to Tennessee, and to Alabama. So much for that promise of international travel. They would bring back polo shirts and jeans from their trips for everyone since we also lived off donated clothes. While my parents and friends' parents were on a mission trip, my friend decided to have sex with her boyfriend of two years. They were 18 and had waited. While his brother and I played cards in the house, she had sex in his truck. Our parents came home after the weekend and heard what happened.

I don't know if she felt pressure to tell or if someone was watching her but that Sunday during church my friend had to stand up and tell everyone that she was a sinning whore who had sex before marriage. She was forced to break up with her boyfriend and she never saw him again. I was furious!!!

I started to rebel. During a shopping trip I wanted a denim mini Guess skirt. My mother said no; it was too tight. I said, "Oh God." She got upset because I was taking the lord's name. I said, "Jeez." Well, apparently "Jeez" is "short for Jesus" and I couldn't say that either. I couldn't win! I decided to start hanging out with a guy who I met when he showed up at the basketball court and pulled a knife out on someone; I was in *love!* Too bad he respected me so much. He was actually a nice guy. He was a nice distraction and drove my fellow cult members crazy just by showing up. I would hop on the back of a motorcycle and ride off property. Every time my parents left I had guys over. Nothing happened *ever,* but I knew the other people would report back to my parents. My dad would ask what happened and when I said nothing he believed me.

While we were there people left, families left but we were told that we were to shun them and to not speak to them because they were going against what God had said and leaving. They were sinners. I was able to sneak and say goodbye to some friends, but some left and I never saw them again. They had a way of manipulating you a little at a time. I saw it happening to my mom and couldn't do anything about it. She really believed that she was following God. We were told that only *their* religion was right, talking in tongs [sic] and all that was the best religion. Baptists were not Christians because being baptized didn't make you a Christian. One of the sayings that they loved was "going to church doesn't make you a Christian any more than going to McDonalds makes you a hamburger."

Catholics were also not Christians and this I heard *everywhere* we went. All the churches said this. Catholics pray to saints and Mary and the idol Mary, but real Christians prayed to *God*. There was more to it than that, but I had gone to Catholic school for a few. Damn, everything I did was sending me to hell.

They started to say that they knew when the end times were coming and that while Jesus sat on the right hand of God, Lew sat on the left. I called it a power trip but everyone else said he was the real thing. The heads of the ministry kept saying they were getting messages from God about what to do with the ministry. One of the rules they—I mean God—came up with was the idea of "Sanctuary." It was on Wednesday night and we basically were not allowed to talk to anyone at all. Total silence unless we were in the house talking to our family. Friends and I would plan the day before to meet and we would hang out...and *not* talk. I always broke that rule. During another parent mission trip three girls and I decided to go to the chapel and listen to music. We blasted Madonna and were dancing. Nothing sexy, this was the early '80s. The chapel was set up so the back was a sliding door that looked out onto a large deck and a beautiful view. During the day you saw the view; during the night you could see yourself. We danced our asses off. The next day I was told that the head of the ministry had walked by and that he had seen us dancing and felt *lust* (we were kids). Dancing was no longer allowed. A poster of Mitch Gaylord, the Olympic gymnast, was ripped off my wall. His hair under his belly button was showing. They said as soon as my dad got home they were going to be talking to him and setting up classes we had to do with our fathers to learn modesty and respect. After each class we had to tell the heads of the ministry what we learned.

My father came home and when I told him what happened he called it ridiculous. He was seeing the hypocrites and seeing how they wanted *everything* for themselves. He went to talk to them and was told that God wanted us to donate all our furniture, dishes, *everything* to them and we were to move to Melbourne, Australia, with just two suitcases each—and our faith, of course. My parents started to get excited about this move, but I was not happy even a little bit. I did one lesson with the dads. Since most were out of town, one dad taught the class for us girls. We were supposed to write the lyrics of our favorite song and bring them in to discuss them line by line and how they were bad. Teaming up with another of my rebellious buddies we pick the worst ones we could. I chose "Sugar Walls" by Sheena Easton. Needless to say the lesson was over before it started. Oh, and I was again told I was a sinner who was going to hell.

Before we were to move, we went back to Florida to say goodbye to my grandparents and the friends I had from when we lived there. This town was my home and if felt like home because although we moved a lot, after we left there we went back for my grandparents. I was halfway through my freshman year in high school. I spent days crying about leaving the country. After the weekend was over my father called me in the living room and asked if I wanted to move to Australia or back to Florida. I said Florida. He said, "Okay then. We are moving back here." He told me not to tell my brother or anyone in Texas when we went back.

We got back to Azle and began packing in secret, hiding boxes in closets. My dad told the leaders we were leaving on a weekday. I went to school that day and apparently word traveled fast. Ministry kids stopped speaking to me. I yelled at one of the girls on the bus to answer me and she said, "YOU AND YOUR FAMILY ARE GOING TO BURN IN HELL. GOD WILL KILL YOU. YOU ARE GOING AGAINST THE WORD OF GOD. On your way to Florida a bridge will collapse and your car will fall in the ocean killing all of you." That was the last I had spoken to any of the kids I knew from there. Late that evening my father drove a U-Haul to our house and the four of us packed all night. At one point my friend's father, my brother's godfather, came over. He didn't say a word but just started picking up heavy stuff with my dad. He hugged my dad and waved, and without a word walked home. The next morning we left. It was the happiest I had been. After we left the head of the ministry's son came out of the closet. As religious as my mom was she always believed that gay people were born that way and had always told me he was gay but keep it quiet and love him anyway. I am glad she was for equal rights. Lew, the leader, had a stroke and was in a wheelchair. Ted Platt, the co-leader's wife, was diagnosed with MS.

Needless to say, we didn't die on the way to Florida, [but] we did break down on a bridge and were stuck there for hours at night. It was then that I realize that some of the brainwashing was rubbing off on me because I was scared. My parents have since divorced. My father has gotten to travel the world: Iceland, Europe a few times, the Caribbean, and Russia with his new wife. He calls the ministry a cult and laughs it off as a bad decision. He goes to church but mostly to network. My mother is working and loves it. She is still religious but very much *not* a doormat and happy. She talks about our time at Azle as a great time with nice memories and says she wouldn't mind a visit back. Some of the families who stayed and left are on her Facebook friends list and it amazes me that they are all still religious. It was so sad and it was worse when one of those people was my mother, who I always loved and respected.

I have a good relationship with her now and when she comes to visit she no longer even asks me to come to church with her. She tells me the paranormal stuff is all demons and that she doesn't want me to talk about it to her but when she has experiences, she calls me excited. She found her own path and it works for her. Her religion—the things she does now—make her a better person. I won't judge her for that. My brother doesn't really talk about it at all but when I say I don't believe in God or a God he says, "You know better than that." Some of the kids that I lived there with are religious, and it's shocking after what happened. Amy, the girl who was forced to announce she was a slut, is extremely involved in her church. She came to visit me once in Atlanta. I shared some memories with her and she said she remembers *nothing*; she said she blocked it out. She said she resents her father but wasn't sure why. Her father has since passed but he was the *only* one who was a true friend to us and he was the one who helped us pack. I will always love him for that. They got to move to Hawaii. Her brother is still there.

I'm in my 40s now and still have a *huge* issue with religion and with people telling me what to do. I know that is because of what I saw and lived in. I saw smart, educated people doing things they would have never done if they weren't brainwashed into doing them. My kids were raised to respect people with different beliefs. They *love* science and evolution. We have friends that are gay, atheist, Christian, Buddhist, and Catholic—gasp—we don't care. I just tell them to question everything! My oldest tells me she doesn't believe in past lives of ghosts. I just tell her to believe what see feels in her heart. I will never force religion on my kids but will support them in whatever they choose. They don't have to believe or not believe in something because I don't. I will always carry some scars from being touched by this cult but I survived and am happy.

Hidden Agenda
By Paul B.

At the close of 1994, my fiancé suggested we hire her brother as a business consultant for our pair of struggling businesses. She told me he had studied with renowned mind researchers John C. Lilly and Jose Silva, among others, and worked with small businesses to increase their profitability. I agreed we needed help, and her brother Don showed up the following spring. His approach was unconventional, but over the course of the summer of 1995, our business issues did improve. His methodology was primarily discussion-oriented, but also employed a modified spiritual framework native to Toltec mysticism. We spent countless hours talking, but also did rituals to "clear the energy" in our workplace. Once the businesses had been restructured, Don left. The businesses both flourish to this day, but the relationship did not. By the end of 1997, Don's sister and I split.

Ten years later, in 2004, I began having dreams about Don and the discussions we'd had that summer in 1995. Huge blocks of information I did not know I possessed emerged in these dreams. Topics like how to craft meaningful agreements, ways to identify and understand anyone immediately by identifying their conscious mindset, how to entrain another's brainwaves using one's voice, and the techniques for programming and early conditioning of the human mind were all coming up. By then I was also a ghostwriter and copyeditor, and thought that many of these topics, properly presented, would make an excellent book. Most self-improvement titles on the market at that time lacked substance. I thought if a book was written giving people complete awareness of their own mind, their behaviors, and the behaviors of others, it would be a game-changer. But if I was going to write that book, I needed more information from the source.

I spent the better part of that year tracking Don down. It turned out he was living in Mexico, having moved his family several times. When I finally sent him an e-mail, he wasn't the least bit surprised. Don said he'd not had enough time that summer to teach me everything I needed to know, so had "sunk it" in my mind, set to blossom into my consciousness when I was "aware" enough to handle it. After a set of fairly lengthy discussions, he convinced me that he should write the book, which I would edit.

It took us into the fall of 2005 until we had a workable manuscript. The final book we produced was quite compelling, as it focused largely on the various ways the soul expresses through the human mind and the myriad ways to clear that pathway.

By then, Don had quit his day job and convinced me he should be teaching classes using our book as the curriculum. I had been attending workshops in neoshamanism, so I knew several people who were interested in such things. I self-published the book at my own expense, signed up eight people for his class in Mexico, and headed south of the border.

Once we were in Mexico, Don became increasingly manipulative with me and the other participants in the class. He began using very intense confrontational tactics, psychological ploys, sleep deprivation, and disorientation, along with a form of hypnotic suggestion, which was delivered using the voice entrainment methods I've mentioned. By the end of that first 10-day workshop, he had set himself up on a pedestal in relation to all the participants and was doing everything he could to make sure we not only wanted, but needed, to please him.

I worked through the spring of 2012 filling his Mexico classes with new students. For those seven years I'd been a true believer in his work, but then I started to realize his methods didn't really accomplish the desired end. Students weren't becoming more soul-expressive; they were becoming more dependent on Don. As time passed, it became clear he was cleverly influencing his students to send him money or do his bidding all under the guise of fulfilling their "purpose." About then he found a well-heeled married couple and a divorced widow with deep pockets willing to cover his bills and finance the further dissemination of his teachings. The couple had been infertile for years, then after Don's classes, they'd had a beautiful baby boy. Don convinced them it was the energy of his agreement with them that had allowed them to get pregnant, despite the fact they had employed a fertility clinic to help them. Another particularly troubling thing he did routinely was convince his students they had been molested, even if they had no recollection of it.

In many cases he purposely planted false memories in their minds to that end.

My final trip to Mexico was a nightmare. By that time, Don was demanding that every single person who came to the classes or who worked with him to "rewrite their programming" end up furthering his agenda. He ignored those who didn't, no matter how badly they needed his help, focusing instead only on those who benefitted him. It was then he explained to me that he'd intentionally used my abilities to further his agenda, and his intent was to continue to use me to set up a chain of floatation tank offices in the U.S. He said customers would come in and float for relaxation, then when they emerged in a psychologically pliable state, his trained staff would rope them into classes, suggesting that rewriting their programming would "fix" them. Never did he encourage his students to find their own expression. They either furthered his agenda or he chased them off.

I left Mexico and never went back, informing Don and his group that I was no longer part of their organization. The backlash was immediate and intense, with screaming threats left on my message machine along with vile e-mails sent to me. Today, Don and his loose group of apostles run six floatation centers in the United States, with more planned for the future.

6

Weapons of Mass Distraction: The Media, Advertising, and Social Programming

Advertising is fundamentally persuasion and persuasion happens to be not a science, but an art.
—William Bernbach

Whoever controls the media, controls the mind.
—Jim Morrison

The media's the most powerful entity on earth. They have the power to make the innocent guilty and to make the guilty innocent, and that's power. Because they control the minds of the masses.
—Malcolm X

The average person sits in front of the television for approximately 34 hours a week, according to a Nielson survey done in 2012. Add to that time spent online or staring into a tablet or smartphone, and it's safe to say most Americans spend at least twice that amount glued to someone else's perceptions and ideas. The mass media is the biggest remote control ever built, and we all exist within the four-walled idiot box it controls.

Manipulation of thought and behavior is a part of our accepted daily lives. Each time we lock eyes on a news story, whether on the tube, the screen, the tablet, or the old-fashioned way, via a newspaper, we are buying into a perspective that may or may not be our own. We read stuff, and readily accept it as reality, often without ever bothering to source the information or take the time to research the subject more deeply. We then pass on some of that information to others, and the viral effect can now, with the Internet and cell phones, travel on a global scale in a matter of minutes.

So if you wanted to truly control the minds of the masses, what better way than buying time on the media outlets the masses most visit? And the most effective types of media most able to manipulate our behavior and change how we think—and even consume? News media, advertising, and, now, social networking.

Get ready to have your channel changed, because with the sheer amount of social programming faced on a daily basis, you are no longer in control of your remote.

Media Manipulation

It's all bad news, all the time. The stories that bombard us on television, radio, and even social networking often tend to be depressing, fearful, and anxiety-provoking—and they spread like wildfire. But we all know that good things happen in the world. Why, then, does the media love to focus on the blood, gore, and violence? Because we respond to it, that's why.

Negative news stories dominate the news because we are hard-wired to respond more to them. It's simple brain science, really, and harkens back to our days of needing every bit of news we could find in order to guarantee our survival. And much of that news involved *fear*. Predators, lack of food and water, bad weather, other nasty humans—our primitive brain responds to bad news because at one time we needed to know it all. Who cared about the good when there was a chance of death around every corner?

Nowadays we face different threats, but we still salivate over and spread the fear. Yet some people wonder if the media is doing this on purpose—propagating fear and anxiety in the masses as a form of mind control. Though possible, and in some cases even probable, they really don't have to work that hard to do it. We take it without a fight.

In his book *Secret Societies and Psychological Warfare*, author Michael A. Hoffman brings up a strong point for the hypocrisy and mixed messages the media sends, especially when it comes to two of the viewing audience's favorite things—sex and violence:

> Have you ever noticed how television and print media will scream themselves hoarse in news documentaries, editorials and heavy analytical pieces about "rising pornography, crime, violence,

gunplay," etc? And yet in the same *TV Guide* announcing the latest special on "The Crisis of Sex and Violence in America" will appear an advertisement for *Miami Vice*, the "show that brings you the action and excitement you've come to expect," etc. Or your newspaper will condemn sex and violence in the loftiest terms but there in the entertainment section is a half-page advertisement for a new "action" movie accompanied by a photo of women in string bikinis and high heels fondling automatic pistols and machine-guns.

Hoffman calls this the "Double-Mind" of mass media, and we are all guilty of buying out of, and right back into, each of the two minds: the one that repels and the one that accepts. The use of images to alter our emotions is an age-old way to manipulate behavioral responses, and the media excels at imagery that shocks us, terrifies us, and titillates us.

For those who believe in mass media mind control, it's easy to find circumstantial evidence of it. Just look at a group of people surrounding a TV set when breaking news announces the latest terrorist attack. Just look at the blank stares of people watching commercial after commercial just to get to their favorite show, which, by the way, they are "addicted" to. News shows, local and national, tell us what they think we need to know, and we buy it hook, line, and sinker, usually without bothering to corroborate the stories ourselves. We trust the media. They wouldn't lie to us, would they? Only politicians and religious leaders do that! Not the talking heads on Fox, CNN, and MSNBC!

Misinformation vs. Disinformation

Much of the information we are bombarded with via a variety of media sources is not corroborated or fact-checked. Many of the news "outlets" people are getting their news from are satire sites, or blogs, or Websites that allow anyone to post a story without having to prove their points or source their material. It's become standard business to spread and take viral the most shoddy reporting, which would never hold up to journalism standards of old, even without bothering to find out who funded the story, who owns the Website it first appeared on, what the source of the information is, and whether or not any other news source has reported on it.

If it's in print, or on the Internet, or the TV, we buy it. Who has time to find out if it's true or not?

Misinformation abounds. This is information that has no basis in fact, or is the result of poor journalistic skills or shoddy reporting. This is information that mistakenly is called fact and gets spread from person to person, network to network, and often goes global before someone decides to finally do a bit of fact checking. By then, it's often too late, as the populace has already accepted the information as valid and real. Even when later presented with facts, it rarely changes the minds of those already entrenched in the falsities, especially if those falsities support their ideologies and worldviews.

Disinformation is planted on purpose, like seeds that will grow into accepted facts. Propaganda, rumor, gossip, news, and fear-mongering all spread with an agenda, usually to provoke fear and paranoia and cause people to react in a specific manner. One night, a news story appears stating that a federal officer was shot and killed by an illegal immigrant, and according to "unnamed sources" the immigrant was a Muslim extremist who snuck across the border screaming about jihad. Before long, anti-Muslim sentiment is spreading across the country, via word-of-mouth, the Internet, and social networking. Three days later, the "truth" emerges: The officer shot and killed an illegal immigrant child that had crossed the border with his parents, looking for freedom.

One must wonder how both stories can exist, with such divergent pieces of information. But it happens every day. Sometimes it happens because we spread news before it is even news—when it is still allegation. Sometimes it happens because "they" cause an event, a cause that will be followed by a desired effect.

Sometimes it's hard to tell misinformation from disinformation, and often the manipulation occurs in a subtle manner on a subconscious level, which makes it harder to pinpoint and, therefore, refute. Lenon Honor, author of *Media Mind Control: A Brief Introduction* and the force behind a 14-hour video series called *How to Decode Media Manipulation*, states on his Website that it comes down to choice and the difference between making a choice, and being led to believe you are making a choice: "While in the midst of the media mind control global apparatus an individual will not realize that they are being subconsciously influenced nor will they realize the sometimes overt, but mainly covert, means of subconscious manipulation present within the media mind control global apparatus." When we are immersed in this apparatus, and we all are regardless of cultural, political, social, or religious differences, we may believe, as Honor says, that we are making choices that are conscious about the direction of our own futures. Yet, we may really be choosing based upon the subconscious programming we've been inundated with over our lifetimes—and not even know we are "under the influence."

One of the main reasons why we allow this is because we are so willingly distracted, Honor states, by the media's idea of what we should know. We would rather spend our time and energy on these distractions than have to face our own truths. He writes, "This subconscious acceptance, in effect, absolves the individual from rectifying their own internal psychological turbulence, for it is easier to focus on distractions that are outside of you than to deal with the mentality that resides within you."

This could easily explain the power of social networking to create its own form of mind control, as more people spend more time on sites that allow for every possible form of distraction.

Facebook and Social Networking

Everyone is on some form of social networking (okay, almost everyone) and nowhere is it more obvious that viral information can be controlled, manipulated, and spread globally in a matter of minutes—even if it's false. Social and peer pressure are rampant as people post away, trying to get approval from their tribe, passing on shocking news headlines, even without reading the actual attached articles. Pictures and images make the rounds, and narcissism is the order of the day. Yet what an incredible forum these sites provide for advertisers and others interested in knowing what makes people tick and what makes them spend.

In 2012, the megalith known as Facebook did something quite nasty to its followers: 700,000 unwitting users were basically utilized as guinea pigs in a social experiment that allowed Facebook to manipulate emotions and emotional responses, without telling anyone it was doing so. Facebook data scientists set out to see if they could influence the emotional state of site users and prompt them to post more positive or more negative content. Using an algorithm that automatically omitted certain content that was either positive or negative, Facebook researchers manipulated users for one week, later publishing their data in the March issue of the *Proceedings of the National Academy of Sciences*. But once the secret experiment got out, people screamed about the blatant invasion of privacy and manipulative, deceitful tactics of the experiment, even causing some of the scientists behind the study to apologize for their less than ethical methodology. Privacy lawyers and organizations came forward, admonishing Facebook for violating the rights of the users, who were never told about the research.

Problem is, Facebook had been doing these kinds of things for years, changing the functions and looks of the site to better serve its users, and give them more access to personal information at the same time. Users just didn't know they were being manipulated until this particular study got attention. The forces behind Facebook understood how easily is was to influence the emotions of users with very little work, and all of it under the radar of the users. Subconsciously, these users were being swayed, even if they weren't consciously aware of anything different on the site during the week of the study. Add to that sites like Twitter, Google, and others being driven by advertising revenue, and there is bound to be a lot of manipulation going on, all for the sake of the sale.

Yet watching television news shows every day we have to wonder if this same level of manipulation is simmering under the stories we accept as "having really happened."

Social Programming

Are we being "programmed" in the same way we program our DVRs to record our favorite shows? Also known as "social engineering," this tactic of politics, religion, and corporate consumerism, even education and academia, involves literally engineering the behavior, attitudes, and desires of large groups of people. Real social engineering is done using specific scientific methods of analysis and decision-making, often for more academic purposes. But social programming goes on every day in ways that are not necessarily meant for the greater understanding of humanity.

We interviewed Ron Patton, executive director of ParanoiaTV and owner of the Paranoia Store in San Diego, about the art of social programming in society.

What exactly is social programming?

Social engineering, within the context of mind control, is a way to gradually and subtly manipulate, coerce, or influence a segment of the population. This is most effectively achieved on the subconscious level. It can also be referred to as form of mass mind control programming.

What entities are behind this, and what might their motives be?

Advertisers, media, politicians, evangelists, and salespeople are the primary entities behind social engineering methodologies and techniques. Their motivation is to attain a desired outcome, whereby the individual or collective group's opinions or decision-making ability is altered for the benefit of the entity and not necessarily for those being subjected to these psychological and sociological manipulations.

The media appears to have an extremely significant influence in re-shaping our thinking, since most television is such a vital part of our society. We usually look to those disseminating information in the media in a professional manner or capacity as "purveyors of truth."

Can you give a few examples of this kind of programming at work that most people would recognize?

The most prevalent would be television via subliminals. Anything being projected onto a screen (movie) or from a computer monitor would also have the same effect. This form of subtle stimuli works below the conscious level (subconscious). Because most of society watches television, it's an ideal delivery mechanism to induce the mind into an hypnotic state. Anything being projected onto a screen, such as a movie, or from a computer monitor, would also produce the same emotional response. Over a sustained period of time, it can create an artificial reality and thus have a profound impact upon society's ability to objectively rationalize.

Neuro-linguistic programming is another example. Also referred as NLP, it's a neurological model encompassing primarily language or linguistics and behavioral patterns. When this process is being used by a skilled NLP practitioner on an unwitting audience, it can make those receiving the multiple stimulus think and do things they normally would not do on a conscious level.

Can social programming ever be a positive phenomenon?

Yes, especially NLP, if applied in such a way whereby we integrate in our lives to achieve positive goals and overcoming negative patterns or addictions. Its original intent was to empower the individual utilizing the various techniques to re-program the brain.

How can we avoid being influenced by this kind of programming?

We need to be educated about the possible ramifications of social engineering, thus, we can more readily discern how it's used and how to overcome its potentially detrimental effects. Of course, some people are more susceptible to this form of programming and must take appropriate counter measures. Individually and collectively, we need to be strong; mentally, by developing a healthy and balanced lifestyle to enhance our critical thinking and mental processing.

Also, if we watch less television or spend less time on the computer, we are most likely not going succumb to the negative influences of subliminals, whether intentional or unintentional.

Control of the masses is the best kind of control to have, and the use of specific techniques to condition and reshape public attitudes is open season to those who understand the methods. This is what makes behavioral engineering of the masses so desirable to authoritarian governments and corporations eager to make massive profits at the expense of the "little guy." A totalitarian governing body can engineer public favor, even as a democratic society initiates a popular "war on drugs" or support for a real war that the country itself has nothing to do with. We might even call the Crusades and the Inquisition successful social programming campaigns. Even Hitler's ability to control the people he ruled over, and get them to accept the most heinous of behaviors, is programming at its most powerful and effective.

It works if you work it, to steal a quote from Alcoholics Anonymous.

Similar to propaganda, social programming is a type of public relations that sways large groups to accept, deny, support, resist, or anything in between. One of the pioneers of public propaganda, known as the "father of public relations," was an Austrian-American nephew of Sigmund Freud, Edward Bernays. Even though he had a degree in agriculture, he was fascinated by the use of propaganda during wartime, and wondered if the same rules and methods could be applied in peacetime as well. He dove headfirst into the world of psychology and public relations, linking the two to design his own concepts of public persuasion and what he called *the engineering of consent.*

By understanding how "group mind" worked, Bernays believed the masses could be controlled and manipulated without being aware of it. He used a lot of his famous uncle's theories in his quest to shift public perception and promote specific behaviors, including his own desire to help out big business by treating the mass distribution of ideas the same way a company would treat the mass production of materials.

Bernays was considered a genius by some, and a threat to free thought by many others who saw his methods as a form of acceptable lies, propaganda with a purpose, and manipulation of the masses for the benefit of the mighty few. His 1928 book, *Propaganda*, remains a highly influential examination of his work and the work of those who came before him, documenting the relationship between what he called an "invisible government, the true ruling power of the country" and the public that was ruled over, something Bernays saw as necessary to keep order over the chaotic masses.

This kind of social control is really about regulating the behavior of both individuals and groups of people in a society, with the influence of propaganda as one of the tools of control. There are both informal and formal methods for doing this. Informal methods might include socialization, cultural norms, and promoting acceptable behavior choices. Formal methods go a step further, using external forces like government sanctions to keep order and regulate, regulate, regulate. Taken to the extreme, formal methods of social control can even include torture as a way of getting people to behave, conform, and calm down.

Media Methods

Some of the methods used by the mass media to control viewers and influence the populace are obvious. Others fly under the radar. All are insidious and are motivated by the desire to reach, and in some way control, the largest audience possible. Those who use the media as a form of coercion know they cannot physically force people to do what they want, buy what they want, and think what they want, so other techniques are employed.

Framing is a means of changing public perception about a subject or concern by imposing a "frame," or base of information, around the subject. This frame doesn't necessarily present false information, but rather accentuates specific positives or negatives of the image presented within the frame. Think of a piece of art that may be very straightforward, at least on the surface, yet changes in the eye of the beholder when surrounded by an ornate frame, opposed to a plain plastic one. The media and politicians use framing as a way of getting people to accept a specific party line of thought surrounding a news story or issue.

To frame an idea is not necessarily mind control, but it is a way to influence thought and behavior. Two completely different groups of people, representing extremes on an issue, can find a way to frame their points of view on the issue that might actually appeal to those in the middle of the road. Framing can make an extreme concept less intolerable, and a tolerable concept more extreme, depending on how it is used.

Similar to framing is paradigm-building. Paradigms are models, patterns of thought and behavior, even tradition. When a paradigm no longer serves a purpose, framing can help reshape the model to be more appealing to more people. The current paradigm may not be one that serves the greater good, but our sociological history shows us that most people will go along with it regardless—until someone, or something, comes along and demands a new paradigm be created. Unfortunately, those who are usually behind the creation of paradigms are the same elite, powerful authority figures behind framing, unless it is an "Anonymous"-style people's revolution.

Language is another great method of swaying public thought and perception. Use of specific words and phrases can literally shape a society's political and religious direction, and create a mentality that is as submissive as the elite in control could hope for. Look at the whole "us vs. them" media assault faced each day with stories of "those black people" or "immigrants" or "feminists" or "the dirty poor" or "the lazy homeless" or "those terrorist Muslims," and it's easy to see how countries can be prodded into accepting violence, aggression, intolerance, bigotry, sexism, and even war. By making someone else the threat, the enemy, the reason behind our problems and the thing to be feared, we can shuck off our own responsibilities and dysfunctions and blame the "other guy."

The more hypnotic and persuasive the language, the more people will fall under its spell. *"We must fight these evil terrorists who wish to steal our freedom." "Freedom isn't free!" "Close the borders!" "Don't let them take our guns!" "The Illuminati controls the world!"* Oh, it goes on and on, yet watch the news for one day and many of these phrases will be evident in the latest fear-baiting story intended to sensationalize and titillate and terrify us into a dull state of shock and awe.

False accreditation is another way of getting people on board an issue or eager to buy a product or serve a purpose. By mentioning "scientific studies" or some vague "10 doctors out of 11," an advertiser or news agency can get plenty of people to blindly accept that a new product is worthy of their hard-earned dollars, or that such-and-such doesn't really cause cancer. Giving credit to science, even when it's false credit, carries a ton of weight with consumers and news audiences, who are too busy and distracted to actually go and research the claims themselves to see if they hold water.

Playing the "Dumb" Card

And that is what makes it so easy for the media, whether it be news-driven or entertainment, to implant thoughts and images and perceptions in the eyes of the beholders. That is what makes it easy for a nation to accept a war with a country that had nothing to do with the terrorist attack it was wrongly associated with, or for a large group of people to take a new drug that has more side effects than benefits, or for a population to give up its own rights to elect a politician who stands against everything they would benefit from.

People have been dumbed down to the point where anything presented as fact, news, or science is accepted without a second thought.

It's that second thought that is so critical, but it doesn't happen often, leaving us reeling, wondering how we got collectively duped again and again.

In "Mass Mind Control Through Network Television," writer/researcher Alex Ansary looks at the role of media in modern times and in our free and civilized society, pointing to the advent of television first, then radio, as ways of brainwashing a population. He writes

> This isn't to say that all things on TV are geared towards brainwashing you. They're not. But most of the programming on television today is run and programmed by the largest media corporations that have interests in defense contracts, such as Westinghouse (CBS) and General Electric (NBC). This makes perfect sense when you see how slanted and warped the news is today.

These conflicts of interest in media ownership now extend to political influence, with conservatives and liberals jockeying for ownership of cable news stations by which they can spread their influence.

Ansary goes on to say that radio also contributes to this brainwashing. Listen to political talk radio and it's clear that your mind is considered an empty vessel in which the talk show hosts desire access to filling! Ansary points to actual changes in the brain that occur when we watch television (zombie brain?), changes that act almost like an opiate and make us addicted to the tube, but also to the many methods utilized to manipulate us into consciously accepting propaganda and disinformation as fact. In fact, he states, "The techniques are increasing in their sophistication over time as the mind scientists that serve the empire continue to discover scientific breakthroughs as to how the human brain functions, learns, retains information, and behaves."

Therefore, the more we learn about the brain, the more we open the door for its manipulation and control by others. Yet, as Ansary warns, "We are given the world reality through a screen, some ink, or radio waves. The truth is hiding in plain site." The problem is, are we smart enough, and paying attention enough, to see it?

If You Can't Beat 'Em, Distract 'Em

Attention is everything, and there are numerous ways to distract a person, and a group of persons. Some of the methods of distraction used by corporations, advertisers, news outlets, politicians, and others include:

○ **Promoting nationalism:** When something happens that threatens our nation, we jump on the patriotic bandwagon, to the point of supporting wars that we cannot afford or getting behind political and religious movements that promote intolerance.

○ **Wagging the dog:** How do you get people to stop focusing on a critical issue? By presenting them with an issue that gets more news time, even if it's trivial and sensationalistic. Someone having an affair? Political scandal? High-powered divorce? Distract them with dirty laundry!

○ **Scapegoating:** Look for the weakest opponent and focus on him or her. The weak link in the chain is enough to break the chain, and is a surefire way to get public eyes off the chain itself.

○ **Misinformation and misleading:** When you want the truth to stay hidden, reframe it with a little bit of falsehood, repeat it often enough until it sticks, and sit back while it goes viral.

○ **Demonizing the other guy:** When we want to take the attention off our own sins, what better way than to focus the public lens on the demons in the other guy? Remember McCarthyism, when people who were against the government's actions were labeled "Commies" and "America-haters?"

○ **Fear mongering:** This is the big one, for what better weapon against common sense and sanity is there than fear, especially hysteria-driven fear? We saw this played out recently with the panic over a few Ebola cases in America that sent the country into a media-driven frenzy of terror and anti-African sentiment.

There are other methods of obvious manipulation, but one of the most invasive is one that occurs beneath the level of human consciousness, where we have no choice in accepting or absorbing it.

Subliminals and Under-the-Radar Mind Control

The use of subliminal imagery and words in advertising is well known by now, and with the advent of the Internet, social networking, and Photoshopping, anyone can create a subliminal meme or message. Heck, we now even have holographic images of dead rock stars, voice changing, and fake videos, and all kinds of manipulation that can occur under our conscious radar. Nothing today is what it appears to be on the surface.

In 1957, a market researcher named James Vicary decided to see what would happen if you inserted words or phrases into a motion picture. Words such as "eat popcorn" and "drink Coke" were inserted into the frames of a movie, just for a single frame and therefore not even long enough to register consciously; it resulted in an increase of sales afterward. Those results were later labeled a hoax, but the concept stood strong and thus the age of subliminals was born, with all kinds of studies, including one at Harvard in 1999, looking at the power of flashing words and images over the subconscious, often with intriguing results. Could you make someone buy a product just by showing a single frame image of a half-naked woman holding the product, even if the person buying it didn't *like* or *need* the product? Could you implant ideas and images directly onto the pliant and impressionable subconscious so easily?

The answer was a definitive yes, and, although controversial, subliminals have been used in product advertising, politics, and even in motion pictures and television shows. Often, television networks or movie companies would claim these were simply glitches or mistakes, but enough of them have surfaced to assure that this technique is well-thought of when it comes to mass mind manipulation via media sources.

One of the most interesting uses of subliminal imagery occurred in the movie *The Exorcist*, where an image of a white-faced demon named Captain Howdy flashes on the screen now and then, despite author William Peter Blatty's outrage against the use of the image in his film. Another involved the 1943 animated Warner Bros. movie, *Wise Quacking Duck*, where Daffy Duck spins a shield. On one frame the words "Buy Bonds" appear on the shield. In one of the most blatant attempts at corporate advertising, an episode of the TV show *Parks and Recreation* titled "Community" contained a scene with a Microsoft logo and stickers. Microsoft just so happened to sponsor that particular episode to promote its new Bing search site.

Most people by now accept that there might be an image of a nude woman reclining in a "come hither" position in the magazine ad they are looking at, or a call to purchase licorice and hot dogs in a few scattered frames of the movie they are watching with their date, but the idea that we are being implanted with images we are not consciously aware of can be frightening indeed, depending on the motives behind the images and the people implanting them.

And the technology to not just insert these images into movie frames or paper adverts, but to literally implant them directly into the brain, does exist. An actual United States Patent, 6,506,148, submitted in January 2003, titled "Nervous System Manipulation by Electromagnetic Fields From Monitors" documents the highly detailed technology available by which, as the Abstract reads, "it is possible to manipulate the nervous system of a subject by pulsing images displayed on a nearby computer monitor or TV set. For the latter, the image pulsing may be imbedded in the program material, or it may be overlaid by modulating a video stream, either as an RF signal or as a video signal."

In other words, the manipulation is no longer just done via a single frame here and there, but by actual modulation of the feed or signal and coming right at you via your home computer, cell phone, television set, or even your DVD player. And the manipulation occurs at a remote source. "For a TV monitor, the image pulsing may be inherent in the video stream as it flows from the video source, or else the stream can be modulated such as to overlay the pulsing. In the first case, a live TV broadcast can be arranged to have the feature imbedded simply by slightly pulsing the illumination of the scene that is being broadcast. This method can of course also be used in making movies and recording video tapes and DVDs."

This is but one patent listed, and the technology is here and now, even more advanced since 2003. Imagine sitting there with your family, watching the evening news, unaware that you are being manipulated with pulsing images originating at some remote location, with the agenda of getting you to accept something, to believe something, to want something—to need something. This is the brave new world of mind control, where there are no shackles and torture chambers, no physical handlers or sinister government agents, no hidden bases or underground chambers needed. It's all done off site, via the electromagnetic spectrum. And you won't even know what's happening until it's too late.

Desensitize the Masses

Perhaps it's all a means of desensitizing the masses to the violence, hatred, and intolerance in the world. Perhaps it's a means of numbing the populace to the realities that they have no power, no wealth, and, really, no say in how the world around them works. By using constant violence, whether on the news or in entertainment shows, and by exposing certain themes of misogyny, racism, and subjugation, eventually the viewing audience comes to accept it all as normal. Desensitization is a powerful way to get someone to go along to get along, even if it means going along to his or her own death and destruction. Break down the inhibitions, expose the brain to constant images that would otherwise be repellant, and hammer the spirit with darkness and death and fear, and you have the perfect consumer, the perfect citizen, numbed to choices and rebellion.

In his seminal work, *Mind Control in America*, Steven Jacobson writes: "The techniques of psychotherapy, widely practiced and accepted as a means of curing psychological disorders, are also methods of controlling people. They can be used systematically to influence attitudes and behavior. Systematic desensitization is a method used to dissolve anxiety so the patient is no longer troubled by a specific fear, a fear of violence for example." Jacobson explains how this process serves to allow the patient—or, in this case, the public—to adapt to situations and ideas that once terrified them, if they are exposed to them enough.

Zbigniew Brzezinksi, when he was National Security Advisor, wrote in *Between Two Ages: America's Role in the Technotronic Era*, "In the technotronic society the trend would seem towards the aggregation of the individual support of millions of uncoordinated citizens, easily within the reach of magnetic and attractive personalities effectively exploiting the latest communication techniques to manipulate emotions and control reason."

Who Owns You?

So, if the media is one big giant mind control tool, who is doing the most controlling of the masses?

Though things change yearly, as corporations rise and fall, here are some of the corporations that literally take up residence in your mind, whether you want them to or not.

The top six corporations control approximately 90 percent of the mass media in this country. Those corporations are (and some of the networks they own):

NBC/Universal: NBC News/Sports, CNBC, MSNBC, Oxygen, SyFy Channel, Telemundo, USA Network, Weather Channel, Focus Features, Universal Pictures, Universal Parks and Resorts, Trio, Paxson, Bravo

News Corp: Fox News, Dow Jones and Company, *The New York Post*, BeliefNet, Fox Business, Fox News, Speed Channel, FX, MySpace, Star World, Star TV India, Star TV Taiwan, DirecTV, 20th Century Fox Entertainment, ReganBooks, Star, Zondervan Publishing, HarperCollins Publishing, National Geographic Channel, News Outdood, Radio Veronica, *The Wall Street Journal*

Time Warner: HBO, Time INC, TBS, Warner Bros. Entertainment, TMZ, New Line Cinema, America Online, Cinemax, Cartoon Network, TNT, *Fortune, Marie Claire, Sports Illustrated*, Castle Rock Films, Moviefone, Mapquest, *People* magazine, Time Warner Cable

Walt Disney: ABC Television Network, ESPN, Disney Publishing, SoapNet, A&E, Lifetime, Buena Vista Home Entertainment, Buena Vista Records, Disney Records, Hollywood Records, Miramax, Touchstone Films, Hyperion Books, PIXAR

Viacom: Paramount Pictures, BET, MTV Canada, Comedy Central, CMT, LOGO, Nick at Nite, *Nick* magazine, TV Land, VH1, Spike TV, Noggin

CBS Corporation: CBS Network, CBS News, CBS Sports, Showtime, TV.com, CBS Radio, CBS Outdoor, CBS Consumer, CW Network, Infinity Broadcasting, Simon and Schuster, Westwood One Radio Network,

Now we have additional powerhouses such as iHeart Radio, Clear Channel, Google, Amazon.com, Facebook, Yahoo!, and Microsoft to contend with as well. The top-10 advertisers chasing after your hard-earned spending money, as of July 2013 (according to AdAge.com), were:

1. AT&T—$1.59 billion
2. Verizon—$1.43 billion
3. Chevrolet—$958 million
4. McDonalds—$957 million
5. Geico—$921 million
6. Toyota—$879 million
7. Ford—$857 million
8. T-Mobile—$773 million
9. Macy's—$762 million
10. Walmart—$690 million

Feel the heat of influence yet? Pop any pills lately? Chances are that Big Pharma influenced your decision as to what pills to pop. The top-five drug advertisers of 2013, according to FiercePharma.com, were:

1. Pfizer—$435 million (Celebrex, Viagra, Lyrica)
2. Eli Lilly—$239 million (Cymbalta, Cialis)
3. Abbvie—$180 million (Humira, Androgel)
4. Merck—$141 million (Nasonex, Gardasil)
5. Amgen—$128 million (Embrel, Prolia)

These amounts don't reflect the billions of dollars in revenues each drug brings in for each of these companies.

So, with so much money and influence consolidated into so few hands, it's easy to see how we don't have nearly as much choice as we think we do when it comes to what we watch, listen to, and respond to with our pocketbooks. The power of the almighty dollar certainly plays a hand in media mind control, but so, too, does the power of putting so much in the hands of just a small number of conglomerates that literally dictate what we call news and entertainment. Yes, we can change the channel, and we can even turn to alternative news and entertainment, we can even turn off the television, the cell phone, and the computer, and sign off the social networking sites, shut off the radio, and stop allowing the voices, thoughts, ideals, and images of others to impose themselves upon our brains.

So who owns you? Ultimately, we can control what we look at and listen to. We can find better outlets for getting our information, and maybe even use our own discernment and source the material that is presented to us as fact. Our minds can only be controlled to the extent that we remain numb, unaware, and distracted.

Once we wake up, take back the remote control of our lives, and begin to program our own minds the way we prefer, and according to our own ethics and goals and values, it gets an awful lot more complicated for anyone else to take up residence there.

7

Mind Power—ACTIVATE!
The Positive Side of Mind Control

It is the mark of an educated mind to be able to entertain a thought without accepting it.

—Aristotle

The mind is everything. What you think you become.

—Buddha

"*Think positive.*"
"*Change your thoughts, change your life.*"
"*Use the power of intention to co-create your reality.*"
"*You become what you think about all day long.*"

We have all heard these motivating quotes in some form or another, urging us to take control of our minds to create the dreams, achieve the goals, and meet the resolutions that we desire. Mind control doesn't have to be a bad thing, and can benefit every aspect of our lives, because, to put it mildly, a mind is a terrible thing to waste. To allow other people, forces, and circumstances to dictate our thoughts, behaviors and reactions is the ultimate form of slavery.

Taking control of our minds is the ultimate act of freedom.

Hypnosis and the Alpha State

The fact that people have lost weight, given up smoking, overcome phobias, and broken through old bad habits and behavioral patterns

155

through the use of hypnosis is a given. Putting the brain in a suggestible and receptive state works wonders for introducing powerful new positive programming to counteract the negative subconscious programming that can keep us stuck in old behaviors and reactions. Even self-hypnosis has become a widely acceptable way of changing one's life for the better.

The use of self-hypnosis as a tool for positive change is a part of a program called the Silva Method, formerly the Silva Mind Control Method, popularized from the 1960s into the 1990s, thanks to many endorsements from top names in the self-help and motivational fields. The Silva Method was the brainchild of an electrical repairman named Jose Silva, who began developing his ideas about the brain, and the use of hypnosis and mind programming in the 1940s. Silva was fascinated with the idea of the split-brain theory, which was later disproven with more cutting-edge research, but his belief that the brain could be influenced in certain brain wave states was foundationally correct.

Using hypnosis, visualization, and mental training exercises and techniques, Silva believed he could increase a person's psychic ability, as well as improve their intelligence, memory, and health by utilizing the alpha brain wave state (7.5–12.5 Hz), which is the state of meditation and daydreaming, a level of awareness that allows for a deeper programming to occur. Silva believed the right brain was the realm of alpha waves and more conducive to increasing intuition, ESP, higher intelligence, guidance, and a much more effective way of influencing the powerful subconscious, where our old programming resides.

Though some of Silva's methods drew criticism and even ire, his followers claimed successes with losing weight, quitting smoking, being happier and healthier, and having more creativity. The key to remember here is that the tools are what cause the change, not the label or name of the method. Hypnosis, visualization, affirmations, and the power of positive thinking have been mainstays of the "new age" of thinking that combines the body with the mind as a unified whole. This holistic way of looking at the human experience focuses on both physical and mental changes working together for the benefit of the whole. Entire books have been written about positive thinking, affirmations, and meditation, so we won't reinvent the wheel here, but all of these are methods of changing the mental and physiological state for a beneficial purpose.

Hypnotherapy combines the use of hypnosis with psychotherapy and is recognized as an effective means of bringing about physical and mental changes, including treating sleep disorders, depression, and even PTSD. There are a number of different types of clinical hypnotherapy, some designed for pain management and others for psychological issues, even addictions, habit control, sports performance, soothing patients before frightening surgeries, and helping people perform better on important tests. But it isn't the hypnosis that is the key, according to Harvard psychologist Deirdre Barrett, who wrote in "The Psychology of Hypnosis," a January 2001 article for *Psychology Today*: "A hypnotic trance is not therapeutic in and of itself, but specific suggestions and images fed to clients in a trance can profoundly alter their behavior. As they rehearse the new ways they want to think and feel, they lay the groundwork for changes in their future actions."

Though it is probably more effective to have someone hypnotize you, for the sake of being able to fully relax into the experience, there are those who use self-hypnosis to improve their lives. Basically, you are putting yourself in a slight trance state, using music or visualization, to achieve a brainwave state appropriate for the task at hand. Alpha brainwaves allow for the mind to focus deeply and imagine a scenario, perhaps guided by a visualization tape, that brings about desired changes to the subconscious programming embedded deep within the recesses of the mind. Zen masters show an increase of alpha waves during deep meditation. Alpha waves are also a part of biofeedback, which hooks a person to an EEG and allows her to take control of her brain waves. Once alpha is achieved, the biofeedback trainer will encourage the person to stay in that state while new ideas and thoughts are introduced, such as overcoming a fear of heights or speaking before an audience. (Ironically, the Department of Defense is exploring biofeedback as a way of getting captured soldiers to create alpha waves, potentially foiling enemy lie detectors.)

Brain Entrainment

Being able to synchronize your brainwaves to an external stimulus is known as brain entrainment. It has become a popular and powerful way to change behaviors and thought patterns, and even bring about altered states of consciousness. Entraining the brain often involves some kind of auditory tool, such as binaural beats, monaural beats, or isochronic tones, that literally put the brain into a trance and achieve alpha, and the deeper theta brain wave state of 4–7 Hz, associated with deep meditation and the realm of intuition and memory. Some people even successfully reach delta, the realm of sleep and the subconscious, at 0–4 Hz. Delta is the "zone" for real re-programming of the mind. Also known as "hemispheric synchronization," the idea is to use specific repetitive sounds or visuals to literally hypnotize the brain and make the brain more open to programming and suggestion (hopefully positive in nature!).

Binaural beats are the most popular for brain entrainment, and occur when two audio signals or tones that are close together in frequency produce a "beat" frequency that is the difference between the two frequencies. When headphones are used, the brain produces the beat or pulse by combining the two "carrier" frequencies, with each ear hearing only a steady tone. The sensation creates a brain that is entrained to the synched frequencies and their beat, which is in the subsonic range. There are a number of affordable machines on the market that produce binaural beats.

Monaural beats are the sum of the waveforms of two tones of the same amplitude that add or subtract from each other, and become louder and quieter in pulses. Monaural beats occur outside of the ear/brain and enter as beats that excite the thalamus and bring about entrainment. Binaural beats combine the two tones in the brain, and monaural beats combine them before they reach the ears. Isochronic tones are manually created tones that are evenly spaced, and turn on and off at a rapid pace. Monaural and isochronic tones do not require headphones, as they occur outside of the brain.

It's all about frequency, amplitude, and modulation, which, when combined in the right speeds, create a hypnotic and rhythmic effect on the brain. But this can be done with visual images such as flashing lights and images, although the deepest entrainment will incorporate an aural effect as well. Think rave dance parties, where flashing strobe lights and rhythmic thumping music put people into trance states. (By the way, the most current research into Stonehenge suggests the site was once used as rave headquarters for our ancestors who wanted to experience altered states of consciousness. But we digress....)

So, if controlling your brainwave states means controlling your mind, once you have that control, what do you do with it?

Thought Power

Can you really change your life by changing your mind? According to the multi-billion-dollar self-help industry, you sure can! Claims abound about how using visualizations, guided meditations, affirmations, and other daily practices designed to put more good data into your mental computer than bad data can really alter the negative influences and forces the mind is subjected to. Garbage in, garbage out, so the saying goes.

Whether you use machines to entrain your brain or a favorite local hypnotist to prime your mind, nothing really matters unless you fill your noggin with more beneficial information designed to bring about real changes. If we truly are being subjected to mind manipulations by our government, politicians, media, and religious leaders, not to mention the narcissists and psychopaths that cross our paths, it does behoove us to fill the well with as much counteractive food for thought as we can.

Though no real scientific studies exist that prove thinking positive will change your life, there is a ton of "circumstantial" evidence in the form of books, movies, television shows, and motivational speakers that will attest to the power of positive thinking. When the mind is pliant and receptive, it is only common sense to suggest that implanting good seeds is far better than bad seeds, as the harvest you reap in the end will be good rather than bad. Personal experiences prove that we perform better, attract more good things into our lives, and just plain feel better when we are in a positive frame of mind. That alone should be cause for keeping a constant watch on our thoughts and what we allow into our minds, from ourselves as well as others.

It's like going to the gym. You can sit there and do nothing, and gain no benefit. Or you can work your muscles on the machines and with free weights, and become stronger and healthier. Same gym, different outcomes, depending on the focus and intention of the gym member. Remez Sasson writes in "The Power of Positive Thinking" of the subtle, yet noticeable benefits of keeping an open and cheery mind: "With a positive attitude we experience pleasant and happy feelings. This brings brightness to the eyes, more energy, and happiness. Our whole being broadcasts good will, happiness, and success. Even our health is affected in a beneficial way. We walk tall, our voice is more powerful, and our body language shows the way we feel."

Other people are affected by our energy and attitude. All of this happens on a deep subconscious level, where we intuitively decide that we either resonate with someone, or get really bad vibes off of them. We broadcast our attitudes, so it is only natural to believe that others are broadcasting theirs, and aligning with people who are broadcasting at the same positive frequencies will bring about success.

But what it really comes down to is this: The mind is a receptacle, as well as a transmitter. It receives as well as broadcasts. Controlling what we allow our minds to receive as well as broadcast keeps out a great deal of information and influence that others around us, from individuals to entities like the government and corporations, would love to instead fill our mind wells with. This is especially important when it comes to the visual symbols and images we allow into our minds. The subconscious is the domain of the symbolic, and understands the meaning of symbols in a manner the conscious mind cannot grasp. Those symbols, if negative, are affecting us against our will and knowledge, unless we are aware of them. Though we cannot directly control our subconscious, we can certainly do so with the many entrainment methods we mentioned, as well as consciously visualizing and focusing on what we want, and not what we do not want.

The basis of the positive thinking movement really comes down to putting better data into the data bank, depositing good energy into the energy bank, and filling the mind with higher thoughts rather than those that depress; create anxiety, fear, and doubt; or diminish our strength, physical and emotional. Affirmations, which are short and powerful statements of intention told in the present tense, repeated often enough, do imprint on the conscious mind, and eventually if said enough and with enough emotional impact behind them, seep down into the subconscious, where they become new programming, replacing the negative programming we grew up with and were exposed to for years and years, without our knowledge or consent.

There are some things science can indeed vouch for when it comes to positive mind control:

- ○ Repetition creates new neural pathways in the brain.
- ○ The subconscious cannot tell the difference between what is real and what is imagined.
- ○ Thoughts backed by strong emotion create stronger neural pathways.
- ○ Brain plasticity allows for constant changes in the brain to occur.
- ○ A repetitive action or thought becomes habitual to the brain after a period of about 21 days.
- ○ Visualizing an outcome effectively programs the brain to achieve the outcome (something many an athlete can attest to!).
- ○ Positive thinking has healed people of terminal diseases.

Deepak Chopra, renowned Indian-American physician and author of numerous best-selling books about quantum physics, healing, intention, and spirituality, wrote in "5 Steps to Harness the Power of Intention": "The classic Vedic text known as the Upanishads declares, 'You are what your deepest desire is. As your desire is, so is your intention. As your intention is, so is your will. As your will is, so is your deed. As your deed is, so is your destiny." The truth is, we are everything we think about all our lives, an accumulation of our thoughts and intentions, manifested outward in our actions. This is what it means to be human. So doesn't it serve us better to keep track of our thoughts and intentions, and make damn sure they are in alignment with who we are and want to be, and not what some external person, place, or thing tells us we should be?

Even if the only thing that ever comes from positive thinking and focused intention is that you sleep better and feel better, the ability to control physiological aspects of your life should be enough to take the subject seriously. We do control our own minds, unless we let in outside influences. Unfortunately, we do let those influences in beginning the day we are born, but once we become adults, we have the ability to change and replace those influences, and avoid new influences from entering our mental space.

So, it naturally brings up the question: If one person thinks positively, what would happen if a million people decided to do so? Collective intention is no longer the stuff of the new age movement, thanks to quantum physics and the concept of a field of potentiality that links and connects everything to everything else. We authors wrote about this field in *The Grid: Exploring the Hidden Infrastructure of Reality*, in which we described it as an implicate level of existence that links a potentially infinite number of realities, with ours being but one level of the Grid that we can experience. Others refer to this collective, unified field as the Akasha, the Zero Point Field, the collective unconscious, the kingdom of Heaven, the Source, the Force, the Universal Field. But the names don't matter.

What matters is that just as we can control our individual minds and behaviors, there is a web of connectivity that allows us to create a "mass control," which can be used for good or for bad, depending upon the intentions of the individuals. Large groups of people thinking the same thoughts can lead to war, and it can lead to peace. Just watch the nightly news and you can tell right away the general intention of the collective with the most influence and power.

Neuro-Linguistic Programing (NLP)

NLP, or neuro-linguistic programming, has been associated with the negative side of mind control and the use of language to manipulate reactions and behaviors, but it also has a beneficial side, according to many people who have claimed it has helped them reprogram their bad habits and achieve specific goals. Although heavily debunked by skeptics who call it a "pseudoscience," NLP has its believers. Like hypnosis, NLP combines neurological processes with linguistics to create a dynamic that changes behavioral patterns. It was created, in fact, as a form of psychotherapy and personal development by Richard Bandler and John Grinder in the mid-1970s. Bandler, a mathematics student, and Grinder, a linguist, modeled their program on the art of changing the brain's programming, much like a computer, with NLP as a manual for the brain.

NLP focuses on three concepts:

1. The study of the structure of subjective experience.
2. Consciousness as made up of a conscious component and an unconscious component.

3. Learning via modeling the behaviors and speech of exemplaries in the desired field.

Though NLP claims to be able to cure illnesses, stop bad habits, eliminate phobias, and change behaviors, even using hypnosis as a tool, there is so much vagueness surrounding the actual concepts and foundations of NLP that the scientific community has chosen to look upon it as another "new age" self-help method.

Interestingly, around the same general time NLP was being developed in the Santa Cruz, California, area, there was a huge human potential movement evolving around the Esalen Institute in Big Sur, California, including Gestalt therapy and a thing called "EST," or Erhard Seminars Training, which was the mastermind of founder Werner Erhard. Erhard held his trainings a few years earlier than NLP, and the influence and intent were obviously a part of the development of NLP. EST proposed to help people transform their consciousnesses and their lives, and improve the income and utilized a mixture of psychology, philosophy, neurology, and behavioral tools, especially the group dynamic that EST became known for (and achieved an almost cult-like status for).

An important part of NLP does focus on using the art of language and persuasion to bring about a desired goal, as well as understanding the ins and outs of communication, none of which is anything new or groundbreaking, except for the way it was packaged in this new dynamic format by Bandler and Grinder. There is also a focus on teaching people how to read other people, namely their body language, which is a tenet of good business practices and certainly a widely studied mode of nonverbal communication useful to people in a variety of enterprises (sales comes to mind).

In the 1980s, NLP was put to the test in a number of strict scientific studies that showed no real benefits from the program, including a research committee study by the U.S. National Research Council that came to the conclusions that there was little if any evidence supporting NLP's effectiveness as a tool for social influence, even though the technique of modeling exceptional people to learn how they succeed at something was considered quite impressive by the committee.

There are people in the world who will tell you they benefitted greatly from NLP sessions with trained practitioners guiding them through the process, even though the NLP claim of speaking directly into the sub-conscious or unconscious mind is only possible through the use of hyp-nosis and suggestive programming. There are people who will tell you it's nothing but bunk/junk psychology. That seems to be the case for a lot of the tools by which people claim to influence, and change, the minds of others.

Our goal isn't to write a self-help tome, or point out how, at the quan-tum level, we are all just a bunch of vibrating particles and waves that await the collapse of the wave function. We have other books that you can read. Our goal here is to remind readers that although negative and sinister uses of mind control have existed since humans began trolling the planet—and still exist—the ultimate form of mind control is evident by how we each live as individuals.

We do have some control. Maybe not total control. But some. It all depends on who we hang around with and where we choose to put our focus. For some people, those choices lead to happy, fulfilling lives. For others, those choices lead to some pretty dark places.

8

GET OUT OF MY MIND!: V2K, ELECTRONIC HARASSMENT, DIRECTED ENERGY WEAPONS, AND TARGETED INDIVIDUALS

> *Voice to skull devices. Non-lethal weapons which includes (1) a neuro-magnetic device which uses microwave transmission of sound into the skull of persons or animals by way of pulse-modulated microwave radiation; and (2) a silent sound device which can transmit sound into the skull of persons or animals. NOTE: The sound modulation may be voice or audio subliminal messages. Acronym: V2K.*
> —From the United States of America's Army "Military Thesaurus"

"Like a nail being slowly hammered the head gets beat. Beaten and beaten till you can't make it. Your brain is being destroyed, bit by bit. Noise in your ears seems to come from contact with microwaves. Implants that respond to microwaves. The RNA structure of your brain is being changed by microwaves, slowly but surely. The clever hypnotist has a hold of you like a washrag. He'll ring you out till your used up! WELCOME TO HELL."

"I began to hear voices in my head and outside my head, which I had never heard before 1974, telling me to do evil things such as kill, steal, lie, cheat, and even to commit suicide. The buzzing sound in my ears began at this same time and is loud enough to drive a man insane. I am NOT insane, yet those friends who have never seen nor heard such things as dozens of voices attacking you at the same time, or endured headaches for months at a time (there is no tumor in my brain), blurred vision, inability to speak correctly (I am a well-spoken, educated lifelong amateur writer studying religious philosophy, world civilizations and societies, etc.) and at times losing balance causing me to walk sideways. These microwave

attacks have increased in velocity in the last five years (I am now almost 70 years of age)...."

"I have been an organized stalking victim for more than 20 years and, like most victims, I'm not sure why. I can only speculate. I've realized that 'they' let you know when you are moving into the next phase of this sick program. For me, it started with harassing phone calls. Then 'they' let me know I was being followed. At that time I also started to experience 'street theater.' Then I noticed friends and neighbors becoming more cold toward me. Chaos began in my family because I was trying to tell everyone about it and they thought I was paranoid (part of the program design). In the beginning, I was very confused and emotional about what was happening to me. Soon I found out about Organized Stalking on the Internet, I was happy to discover there was a name for the madness and began researching it. It has helped me to stay sane. 'They' know they cannot break be down psychology. I think that is one of the reasons the electronic harassment started. In 2001 I experienced my first V2K transmission and I have been harassed with various forms "non-lethal" technology since then. We TIs need to spread the word so that EVERYONE will understand that this really does happen."

These individuals are not alone. They claim to be among hundreds, possibly thousands, of TIs—"targeted individuals" who are being electronically harassed, beamed with direct energy weapons such as microwave blasts, gang stalked, and victimized with a technology called V2K (voice to skull) that literally makes them hear things in their heads. And the scary thing is, for every claim, there is a patented technology to back it up.

The world of non-lethal weaponry has opened the door to such technologies that allow the control of one's mind, thoughts, actions, and behaviors from afar, via the use of sound, heat, and light. The electromagnetic spectrum offers the possibility of using pulsed high-frequency microwave blasts, electrical transmissions, and sound waves that can bypass normal inhibitors and enter the human body and brain, either directly or indirectly—and unbeknownst to the person being targeted, until they begin to suffer the dire consequences.

And it's been going on for decades.

Voice to Skull

In 1973, Dr. Joseph Sharp of the Walter Reed Army Institute of Research successfully demonstrated "voice to skull transmission" using artificial microwaves, by using a computer to control a radar transmitter sending out a single pulse that was heard inside a test subject's head as a "click." These pulses, and therefore clicks, were actually entrained to the timing of the human voice waveform, which then resulted in a voice being heard directly inside the head, rather than a series of clicks. His brilliant, if not disturbing, research was published in the March 1975 issue of *American Psychologist*. Continued research into the use of microwaves and behavior modification found academic attention in 1975 when Dr. Don R. Justesen published an article titled "Microwaves and Behavior" in the March volume of *American Psychologist*," laying a larger foundation for the use of pulsed microwave radiation as a method of controlling people, as in wartime or riot situations. Justesen wrote that the sounds heard "were not unlike those emitted by persons with an artificial voice box (Electro larynx)." He also wrote that the sounds heard were simple words, not complex, as more complex words would require more energy to transmit and possibly approach or surpass the limit of safe exposure. Along with colleagues he went on to develop a receiver less/wireless voice transmission system for ARPA, the Advanced Research Projects Agency.

But this was not new thought, for as far back as 1962, the use of what is known as the "microwave auditory effect" was being explored and discussed in the world of neuroscience, with American neuroscientist Allan H. Frey being the first to publish in the *The Journal of Applied Psychology* in 1962 (Volume 17). In fact, his name was tagged onto the phenomenon, often referred to as the "Frey Effect." As far back as 1968, patents for devices that used different methods of exciting brain waves and the nervous system with the use of sound, microwaves, and the electromagnetic energy pulses were filed, including one granted in July 1968 called a "Nervous System Excitation Device." Clearly, it was only a matter of time before military applications were found for this technology, and the crux of interest resulted in a series of experiments and classified projects throughout the next few decades, examining the use of microwave auditory effects as a means of non-lethal warfare and crowd control weaponry.

Non-Lethal Weapons

In December 2006, one such program was declassified as a response to a Freedom of Information Act request. "Bioeffects of Selected Non-Lethal Weaponry" proved that our own government, and our military, knew of the potential of applying microwave auditory effects as a non-lethal way of disrupting behavior without the victim even knowing what hit him or her, or where it came from. For those on the front lines in war, and those on the front lines in the law enforcement field, that kind of weaponry was priceless. One could disable criminals or enemy combatants without actually killing them. The FOIA documents included the following statement: "Microwave hearing may be useful to provide a disruptive condition to a person not aware of the technology. Not only might it be disruptive to the sense of hearing, it could be psychologically devastating if one suddenly heard 'voices in one's head.'"

Imagine claiming to hear voices, clicks, and sounds inside your skull and trying to tell someone else about it. The consensus would be that you were mentally ill or on drugs. It's the perfect method to drive someone slowly mad, or psychologically and physically disable him or her, and never let on who or what is behind it.

This of course made it the ultimate weapon for military purposes, inciting even more research into systems that could remotely incapacitate people, even if only temporarily. In 2003, the U.S. Navy conducted research with a system called MEDUSA, which stood for Mob Excess Deterrent Using Silent Audio, and focused again on the use of modified microwave pulses to cause such great discomfort to personnel entering a specific area or protected perimeter.

Stalked and Harassed

According to targeted individuals or TIs, the remote manipulation of the body and mind by various advanced technologies, even weapons, is happening every day. These individuals claim they are victims of electronic and directed energy harassment and report a list of symptoms they claim to suffer:

○ *Burning sensations on skin or internally.*

○ *Pinprick sensations over skin and in extremities.*

○ *Extreme headaches.*

○ *Extreme fatigue that comes on suddenly.*

○ *Visual hallucinations.*

○ *Mysterious skin problems.*

○ *Uncontrollable body movements; twitches.*

○ *Voices of people in mind (V2K, or voice to skull) when no other people present; can also be animal sounds.*

○ *Sounds of footsteps inside, outside, or on roof of your home when no one there.*

○ *Sounds that are not identifiable and feel surreal in nature.*

Being "gang stalked" or experiencing "organized stalking" is another common claim from targeted individuals who are being harassed. The idea is to create fear, intimidation, and confusion in the victim(s). Methods used include:

○ *Brighting: People turn their headlights on you wherever you are.*

○ *Stalking: Being followed by cars and pedestrians, sometimes very obvious; people even report planes flying over in patterned intervals.*

○ *Mobbing: Suddenly being surrounded by people, when walking or in your car.*

○ *Noise harassment: Neighbors suddenly become very noisy at all hours.*

○ *Objects: People leaving strange objects in your yard; workplace, automobile, personal objects destroyed.*

○ *Privacy: Computers hacked and other invasions of privacy breached.*

○ *Discrediting: People suddenly smear campaign you, via slander, libel, and social networking attacks, even so far as accusing you of child molestation, crimes, etc.*

Signs of being gang stalked include:

○ *The sense of being watched and followed.*

○ *Rude behavior directed at you by strangers.*

○ *Hearing bits of private conversations you've had coming from strangers around you.*

○ *Vandalism and signs of repeated break-in attempts at your home or office.*

○ *Sudden strained relationships with friends, lovers, colleagues.*

○ *Frequent auto accidents and unusual repairs.*

○ *Objects around home moved around.*

These tactics have often been compared to the types of psychological warfare used by the Nazis, the KGB, and cults to cause extreme fear in the victims to possibly keep them from whistle-blowing or exposing secrets and information they might have against the perpetrators. Some targeted individuals, though, have no idea why they are targeted, which suggests perhaps they are just unfortunate chosen guinea pigs for mind control experimentation and behavioral modification.

Law enforcement has been using non-lethal weapons to quell crowds and keep riots under control for years, including LRAD—the Long Range Acoustic Device, which used sound waves to cease violent behavior by temporarily disorienting the intended victims. These devices serve useful and easily identifiable purposes for both military and law enforcement, but there exists a more insidious and much less practical use for this kind of technology. According to TIs, who are coming out in public via online forums and Websites, organizations for mind control victims, and various books and even movies, people are being "pulsed" with V2K technology by those they refer to as the perps (those who are pulsing the targeted individuals), and often have no clue why.

As psychologists scramble to identify these victims as mentally ill or delusional, the victims themselves insist otherwise. There are those who believe that V2K may be a real hazard to their health, and have all the recorded and documented ailments to prove it. According to TIs experiencing V2K in particular, some of those symptoms or effects include:

○ The sound of clicking "Morse Code like" and actual voices inside the skull.

○ Muscle vibrations and "humming."

○ Tinnitus and clogged ear ways.

○ Sinus issues and allergies, throat irritation, and body aches.

○ Actual rashes and "burns."

○ Dizziness, confusion, and vertigo.

○ An out-of-body sensation, or a sensation of not being in physical control.

○ Increase in autoimmune diseases and even cancer.

Though the presence of any or all of these symptoms doesn't mean a person is automatically under mind control or even V2K, many of the TIs also report phone harassment, being followed, "gang stalking" (which we will get into soon), cyber stalking, electrical and computer issues in their homes, cell phone interference, and eventually a strong sense of paranoia and disorientation. Some TIs can identify potential ties to people they know who may be under surveillance, such as corporate and government whistle-blowers or activists. But many TIs cannot figure out their connection to any situation or person who might account for the harassment they are experiencing, and conspiracy theorists suggest that perhaps people are being targeted in general as "guinea pigs" for the testing and advancement of this type of technology.

Mind Games

Sounds like a cool plot for a science fiction movie, but it may actually be happening. In a January 2007 story called "Mind Games" in the *Washington Post*, reporter Sharon Weinberger interviewed a TI named Harlan Girard, who confessed at the age of 70 that he had been experiencing ongoing government mind control and harassment, possibly because of his ownership of some sensitive declassified national security documents that proved our own government was developing weaponry "that send voices into people's heads. It's undeniable this technology exists," Girard told the reporter, "but if you go to the police and say 'I'm hearing voices,' they're going to lock you up for psychiatric evaluation."

Girard claimed his problems started in 1983 when he was a real estate developer in the Los Angeles area, first with subtle harassment and strange happenings, including his neighbors watching him. He also experienced people running under his windows at night and even entering

A Long Range Acoustic Device used onboard the USS Blue Ridge during a small boat attack drill, 2006. U.S. Navy image.

his apartment crawlspace. Then the harassment stopped, only to start up again a year later, and much stranger. This is when he began to hear voices and he could actually distinguish differing male voices. According to the article, "The voices were crass but also strangely courteous, addressing him as 'Mr. Girard.'" The voices taunted him and suggested that he was going crazy, which led Girard to ask his psychologist girlfriend at the time if it was possible. She thought not.

Soon, the voices were constant, creating chaos in his brain accompanied by severe pain all over his body—which Girard now attributes to directed-energy weapons that can shoot invisible beams.

Though Girard did not have a smoking gun document among those he believed caused him to become a TI, he did have enough to show that V2K and mind control were, and are, on the minds (pun intended) of our military and government officials. Thus, the onus of proof falls upon the victims, many of whom are highly intelligent, functioning people with jobs in high places and great reputations.

They just happen to hear voices in their heads.

Often, men and women like Girard report electronic assaults on their sexual organs. "My testicles became so sore I could barely walk," Girard states of an early experience with such an assault. Women, such as Susan Sayler of San Diego, report electronic sensations to their sexual organs that are not related to any kind of sexual encounter with the opposite sex, or even muscle spasm.

Gloria Naylor, a renowned writer and author of *The Women of Brewster Place* came out of the closet of sorts in 2005 when she published a book called *1996*, a semi-autobiographical account of her own experiences as a targeted individual. She wrote about hearing conversations in her head while lying in her quiet Brooklyn brownstone bedroom, or the "street theater" she was subjected to—a form of organized gang stalking. She was followed, noticed strange cars driving past her isolated vacation home, and even experienced such chilling things as having people mimic her movements on an airplane. Naylor sought psychiatric help, and was put on anti-psychotic drugs, but the voices in her head continued. Interestingly, the voices and other activity seemed to stop around the time Naylor discovered online mind-control forums.

Lest you think Naylor is alone in her claims, another great 20th-century novelist, Evelyn Waugh, wrote about street theater gang stalking in a book called *The Ordeal of Gilbert Pinfold*, written a few years after Waugh had his own such episode, one he ascribed to a drug-induced hallucination.

Psychiatrists and other therapists who see patients claiming to be TIs often have to struggle to separate these extreme experiences from pure paranoia, hallucinations, schizophrenia, and just plain mental problems, including attention-seeking. But many in the field are compelled to suggest that some of these TIs are having honestly chilling experiences that they truly believe are not psychosomatic or physiological in origin. Still, many, such as Scott Temple, professor of psychiatry at Penn State University, feel that the individuals who suffer what he calls auditory hallucinations are simply overwhelmed by the experiences and combined with a lack of insight into their illness, create delusional interpretations associated around the events. Another psychologist, Harvard's Susan Clancy, noted that the stories she hears of TIs are often remarkably similar to those of people claiming to have been abducted by aliens: strange pains; the sensation of being watched, followed, and targeted; as well as the belief that their thoughts are controlled via implants.

The idea of implants that can be put into the body to control the mind is not just the stuff of espionage movies and science fiction, though.

In "A Game of Tag," published in the May 2011 issue of *Fortean Times*, reporter David Hambling looks at implants and electronic harassment. He interviewed a man named James Walbert, who claims to have an electronic device embedded in his shoulder that tracks his every move. It also gives him severe muscle contractions. Walbert believes the implant was put in him to track and control him from a distance. Walbert, who is from Wichita, Kansas, and not involved with any government or military organizations, or drug cartels, even went so far as to have a local doctor clear him of mental illness. He also had an expert in technical surveillance, William J. Taylor, run a scan on his body with two portable radio frequency detection devices. A low signal was indeed found to be coming from Hambling's right upper back area, which turned out to be low bandwidth, around 288MHz, the VHF band used in commercial television, radio, and other transmissions.

It's also the band reserved for military use in the United States.

An MRI showed the exact source of the scan, which was then shown to a Dr. John Hall of the Spine and Joint Institute of Texas, who stated in the article that the scan was "clearly showing a capsule-shaped foreign body in his right trapezius muscle." Hall states that he has seen many patients who believe they are TIs of this kind of implant harassment.

Tracking Targeted Individuals

Other TIs claim to be victims of more unusual forms of identification and tracking techniques, such as the Smartwater Index Spray System, courtesy of the security company Smartwater. This product, according to the company's Website, can spray a person with a water-based solution, which contains a unique "forensic code." Though this kind of product is normally used to link a criminal with a crime scene, its ability to tag a person with the spray, which shows up under ultraviolet light, could certainly be misused for other purposes by any agency that wanted to keep tabs on someone.

In a sense, tracking someone, especially when she is aware of it, is a form of mental manipulation designed to create fear, paranoia, and weakness in a target. Mind control is not just about brainwashing and programming, but also making someone so frightened that he willingly changes his behavior to avoid that which is making him afraid. Or at least insane.

Often, V2K victims will pass of the voices as their own thoughts, or believe they have schizophrenia. Some might indeed even doubt their own sanity. But to the truly targeted, they know the difference. Some suggest that they've actually been hypnotized via the voices and possibly subliminal commands being "downloaded" into their skulls. This type of programming smacks of the mind control uploading of the cold war era and classified MKUltra projects, discussed earlier in the book. V2K may be a more modern technology, but the goal is the same as it ever was: to reprogram a person's mind, and control it, as well as that person's actions, thoughts, and behaviors.

A TI by the name of Eleanor White describes it as "psycho-electronic mind control," a covert, around-the-clock harassment that includes electronic mind and body attacks, including V2K. *Psychotronics* is another word used to describe the kind of electronic harassment that infringes upon the civil liberties of the victims, and their privacy and control of their own thoughts. The manipulation of human beings by using electronic means to affect and influence their minds, thoughts, psyches, and behaviors using any number of means, whether subliminal, visual, auditory, or through directed energy right into the brain, falls under the umbrella of psychotronics. The subject, while usually receiving the usual tin-foil-hat response from most people, is indeed to be taken seriously, as more and more evidence of actual research studies, conducted on behalf of our own government, as well as the governments of other nations, comes to light.

Take, for example, the USSR government experimenting with the induction of sleep by means of radio waves, which was registered as "Radioson," or Radiosleep with the Government Committee on the Matters of Inventions and Discoveries. Imagine being able to knock someone into dreamland with a radio wave or microwave pulse, one that he has no idea is coming at him, and from where. Many such patents and inventions exist, and are documented on a variety of Websites devoted to shedding light on this dark corner of human research and mind manipulation (usually these studies are directed at either military or law enforcement agendas) on behalf of governments, military organizations, and even private corporations interested in keeping one step ahead of the competition.

Not to keep picking on Russia, because the United States is just as active in pursuing these types of weaponry to keep up or keep ahead, but in April 2012, several news stories, thought at first to be April Fools' jokes, revealed that Russia was working on an "electromagnetic radiation gun" that would attack the central nervous system and render a human being into a zombie state. The articles, which appeared across a variety of sources, including the *Herald Sun*, went on to state that the guns use electromagnetic radiation similar to that found in a microwave oven and are being developed for future use against the nation's enemies and even dissidents within. The hope was these guns would be workable and ready for field use by 2020.

In his book *Psychotronic Golgotha*, N.I. Anisimov, a Russian author and expert on Russian psychotronic mind control, states:

> At the dawn of the scientific-technical progress, dictators and rulers of totalitarian governments dreamt about how to embody the most ancient occult sciences and hidden potentials of mankind's psyche in technical weapons in order to, with their help, make their own populations obediently conformist, blindly fulfilling the wishes of the dictator and his associates.
>
> They even cherished monstrous ideas, after the creation of super-weapons, of using these for the enslavement of other governments and of becoming rulers of the world. With the creation of such types of weapons the military has been receiving the ideal weapon of mass enslavement and destruction, and the Secret Services an ideal zombie agent capable, without portable radio sets and guns, of obtaining and conveying secret information. But if at the end of the past century, the embodiment into life of these dreams—given the weak development of technology—was not possible, then already by the start of the 20th century, when scientific-technological progress was becoming intensively developed, these dreams came to be realized into practice.

Anisimov refers to these "humanitarian weapons" as the plague from the 20th century, which will no doubt see fruition in the 21st century as technology advances. He writes:

Their invisible components can:

○ kill at a distance, imitating or causing any chronic illness

○ they can make a person a criminal or irresponsible

○ create aviation, railroad, or automobile accidents in a matter of seconds

○ destroy fundamental structures

○ destroy, create, or provoke any climatic cataclysm

○ control the most complex instrument or mechanism

○ control the behavior of people and any biological object

○ change the world-view of the population.

The scary fact is: These technologies exist, and they can manipulate a person or a number of persons from a distance without any warning or knowledge. With little control and transparency, who is to say these inventions and devices are not being used on civilians outside of any law enforcement emergency or wartime necessity? There is no government oversight, and the subject matter gets shoved under the "conspiracy" rug. Yet what is a conspiracy but an attempt to conspire to do something in secret?

Directed Energy Weapons

Another way to describe this kind of cranial harassment is called *directed energy weapons harassment*. Directed energy weapons can include any kind of directed energy, whether in the form of light, sound, heat, electrical, or kinetic, at a specific target or person. These types of devices are not new. The Russian LIDA Machine, which uses EM pulses to make a target exhausted or sleep deprived, is said to have been in use since before the 1980s. CNN ran a special report in 1985 on the work of one Dr. Ross Adey, who studied the LIDA Machine and appeared on the show with one. LIDA can pulse not only sound, but also light and even radiant heat, but usually only with a patient or person in close proximity. However, Adey and a colleague, Dr. Eldon Byrd, were also studying the LIDA for possible potential as a weapon! Many TIs insist this type of machine might account for one of the worst symptoms they suffer—incredible fatigue.

Some of the symptoms or indicators of a directed energy weapon attack allegedly include:

- Sudden waking at exactly the same time at night, as if prompted by an external force.
- Hot stinging or needling sensations deep within the flesh, especially while attempting to sleep.
- Vibration of muscles and body parts or nearby immobile objects.
- Fast and pounding heartbeat and ringing in the ears.
- Very high body heat despite cool surroundings and lack of actual fever.
- Sudden and extreme fatigue.
- Evidence of break-ins and disruptions to home and workplaces.
- Possible phone or home bugging and tapping.
- Systematic traffic down street or cars parked regularly that do not belong on street.

Whereas someone who is not experiencing these symptoms or effects might suggest extreme paranoia, to those who are trying to put the pieces of the puzzle together, it becomes obvious that they are being targeted for some reason and punished with systematic harassment by a variety of insidious and distressing means. One of the key statements made by TIs is that their homes are often broken into, but nothing is ever stolen. Many report coming home to find locked doors opened, or garage doors opened, but nothing taken or destroyed, as if the perps wanted only to frighten and disturb the TIs, not actually harm them.

Pop, Click, Buzz, Talk!

United States Patent #4,877,027 was filed by Wayne B. Brunkan in June 1988, and given patent approval in October of 1989:

Patent for Microwave Voice-to-Skull Technology—Abstract

Sound is induced in the head of a person by radiating the head with microwaves in the range of 100 megahertz to 10,000 megahertz that are modulated with a particular waveform. The waveform consists of frequency-modulated bursts. Each burst is made up of ten to twenty uniformly spaced pulses grouped tightly together. The burst width is between 500 nanoseconds and 100 microseconds. The pulse width is in the range of 10 nanoseconds to 1 microsecond. The bursts are frequency modulated by the audio input to create the sensation of hearing in the person whose head is irradiated.

This particular patent, which is one of many involving such technology, contains highly detailed descriptions of how to make the device, as well as graphs and drawings. Basically, the invention patented allows a pulsed signal on a radio frequency carrier of approximately 1000MHz to effectively create "intelligent signals," as the inventor states, "inside the head of a person" when the electromagnetic (EM) energy is projected through the air towards the person's head. The inventor goes on to state that the bursts or pulses cause "increasing ultrasonic build up within the head of a human being starting with a low level for the first burst pulses and building up to a high level with the last bursts pulses of a group." The buildup of pulses is thought to create the direct discharge of random neurons in the brain, creating a perception of sound.

Although this patent holder had not actually tried his own invention out, the work of Dr. Allan Frey, and Dr. Joseph C. Sharp and Mark Grove, who performed the first successful classified experiments with V2K in 1974 at the Walter Reed Army Institute, found that single microwave pulses can be heard by some people as pops or clicks, and a series of uniform pulses can be a buzz, and all without any kind of receiver. This is called microwave hearing, and by discovering the right carrier frequencies and proper pulse characteristics, actual intelligent words and speech are created.

Directed energy beam weapons use light and radio waves as their chosen form of ammunition. The U.S. military has been exploring this pulse energy weaponry for decades, according to a July 2005 article titled "Despite Promise, Energy Bean Weapons Still Missing From Action." The article states that these pulses, which behave much like the phasers in *Star Trek*, can provide a precise, instantaneous, and inexhaustible form of firepower on future battlefields, if the technology is ever logistically realized. James Jay Carafano, a senior fellow at the Heritage Foundation, a conservative think tank, stated, "It's a great technology, with enormous potential, but I think the environment's not strong for it." Carafano felt not enough money and time was spent perfecting directed energy weapons, but suggested it be a high priority. This could be because the target, whether a human or object, cannot avoid being hit by the beam, because the beam moves at the speed of light. The beam can even penetrate walls at certain frequencies. It's a military dream come true in terms of fighting power and precision.

Right now, there are some directed energy weapons, so to speak, such as hand-held laser devices that can be used to render someone temporarily blind, which were utilized during the Iraq War. One such system, the Active Denial System, developed by the Air Force and built by the Raytheon Company, can produce millimeter-wavelength bursts of energy, capable of penetrating 1/64th inch into human skin. That is enough to agitate water molecules in the dermis and produce heat, a sensation strong enough to stop a person from whatever he or she is doing.

Non-lethal directed energy weapons may be the stuff of future battlefield strategies, but for many targeted individuals, the same systems and technologies are already being used to control, manipulate, terrorize, and harass citizens off the battlefield.

The Jesus Mendoza Maldonado Story

One of the most fascinating and chilling accounts of a targeted individual comes to us from Texas. A man named Jesus Mendoza Maldonado has meticulously documented ongoing electronic and microwave harassment, gang stalking and other forms of harassment and surveillance, as retaliation for Maldonado's whistle blowing. Through his own writings, the actual legal court documents, and a series of YouTube videos, Maldonado tells his story, even as his health fails from years of microwave bombardment. He has gone to the highest levels of government to try to stop the harassment, including the CIA, with his own account of the ongoing horrors he and his family face. His case even went as far as the U.S. Supreme Court, where it was dismissed.

In the actual lawsuit first filed in a federal court on behalf Jesus Mendoza Maldonado, some of the matters on the court record included:

23. At several times relevant to this case, the intensity of radiation has impaired plaintiff health condition during State administrative hearings in which plaintiff has been seeking rehabilitation services.

24. At several times relevant to this case, the intensity of the electronic aggression has increased when plaintiff explains to others the discriminatory motive of the electronic aggression.

25. At several times relevant to this case, plaintiff's three-year-old son and four-year-old daughter suffered pain with convulsions when a meter showed high intensities of radiation inside plaintiff's home.

26. At several times a microwave meter has detected several beams merging on the head of plaintiff's three-year-old son.

27. At several times relevant to this case, plaintiff's three-year-old son has collapsed crying in pain when a microwave meter has shown several beams merging on his head.

28. At several times relevant to this case, plaintiff has recorded on videotape the electronic aggressions.

29. At several times relevant to this case, a microwave meter has shown several beams merging on the bed of plaintiff and on the bed of plaintiff's children.

30. At several times relevant to this case plaintiff's children have complained of pain when intense radiation has been found inside plaintiff's home.

31. At several times relevant to this case plaintiff's children have suffered convulsions while asleep.

Maldonado's documents on his blog (http://jesusmendozza. blogspot.com) *his battle with the courts over the recognition of his suffering at the hands of the defendants in the case, who utilized gang stalking and microwave harassment directed toward him and his family. He writes: "I was maliciously overexposed to radiation for the first time in 1997, as retaliation for denouncing a fraudulent scheme against the second largest law school in the country, the Thomas M. Cooley Law School located in Lansing, Michigan. At that time I was going on my second year of law school."*

Maldonado then found himself in the ER with a swollen heart and breathing difficulties, which he states happened just a few days after submitting evidence to the dean of the law school that the school was engaged in racial discrimination, fraud of federal funds, and the giving away of law degrees to those affiliated to government agencies.

Maldonado claims that the electronic and microwave harassment he experienced when he was on the Dean's List forced him to leave the school before he could finish his last semester and return to Mission, Texas. He left the law school in good moral and academic standing, and sought help from the federal courts. Although the litigation failed to stop the electronic aggression against him and his family, the lawsuits established a record of legitimacy of his claims.

In 2003, Maldonado filed suit against then–U.S. Attorney General John Ashcroft to put an end to the electronic aggression, which he claimed was affecting his children's health. He had proof in the form of detection equipment showing high intensities of radiation inside his home in Mission, Texas. In February 2007, Maldonado filed suit with the United States Supreme Court when his three children became sicker, showing signs of heart abnormalities, disorientation, swelling in the face, speech issues, and one of his children even growing a tumor on her foot.

> *To this day, Maldonado has gotten no justice for his exposure to this kind of targeted harassment. He has not blogged since 2008.*

Though many targeted individuals seek help from a psychiatrist or psychologist, only to told they are "hearing things," the past use and present patents and applications of this kind of technology in military and law enforcement settings makes it a little easier to believe that perhaps, indeed, these people *are* hearing voices—actual voices—inside their heads.

Shielding

Is there any way to stop this kind of insidious invasion of the mind? Shielding is suggested on many TI forums as a means of diverting or protecting oneself from microwave, electronic, and V2K harassment.

Shielding techniques include:

- Wearing leather to help against microwave attacks.
- Wearing rubber gloves, shoes, caps, and boots to offset electrical sensations.
- Repeating positive "mantras" during attacks to offset paranoia and fear.
- Avoiding psychiatrists and other healthcare professionals unless they are known to be open-minded about TIs.
- Keeping busy and exercising to keep healthy and offset the physical harm of attacks.
- During V2K episodes, turning up music or television loudly, or going outside and being around noises to offset voices and pulses.
- Using therapeutic magnets and clothing designed to offset electromagnetic energy.
- Avoiding locations where gang stalking and street theater have occurred before.
- Wearing earplugs to stop externally projected sounds.

Of course, there are many companies ready to sell you a lead suit or a tin-foil hat (yes, they actually may serve a real purpose!) for a price, but there are a plethora of TI Websites and forums with victims willing to provide insight, experience, and support to anyone claiming to be under the assault from these sinister and enigmatic forces.

Not everyone who thinks they are a TI actually are. Many people can figure out why they might be targeted. Some invent something that might upset the corporate world or oil industry; others whistle-blow; others may be related to individuals in the military or high government office. But a number of TIs are ordinary people with no apparent links to anything that might even suggest they are a potential target for si-lencing and controlling—and that is what makes this all so frightening. Because if even a small percentage of these TIs are truly being targeted by this new and cutting-edge technology, it means any of us could be, and that we don't even have to have done anything more to deserve it than breathe.

Elana Freeland, author of *Chemtrails, HAARP and the Full Spectrum Dominance of Planet Earth*, writes in "This Covert Electromagnetic Era: Directed Energy Weapons (DEWs) for Political Control" of the long his-tory and the current concerns of this technology, and how it is being used on us in secretive ways that have nothing at all to do with fighting terrorism:

> It doesn't take a rocket science degree to see that remote sat-ellite tracking and over-the-horizon technologies are not just about "terrorists." Remote torture and interrogation, memories triggered by neurophone questioning, and brain wave analyzers delivering "forced conversations" and programming are bout the establishment of electronic POW concentration camps in our homes and workplaces. They're about mental rape and intellec-tual property stolen right out of our heads. The silent, invisible, improvable uses such weapons can be put to us is mind-boggling.
>
> We could all be potential guinea pigs.

"A game of chess, a chase of sanity'—one targeted individual indicated that the whole harassment/targeting is a 'mind game.' The perpetrators

main goal is steal your sanity. They want you to know they are there. They want your undivided and constant attention. In short, they want you to be paranoid and delusional. You have to learn to block them from your consciousness. Do not give them gratification."

—From "Targeted Individuals 101" Survival Guide

9

SOMEBODY'S WATCHING YOU: THE UNITED STATES OF SURVEILLANCE

We are moving rapidly into a world in which the spying machinery is built into every object we encounter.
—Howard Rheingold

I can't in good conscience allow the U.S. government to destroy privacy, Internet freedom, and basic liberties for people around the world with this massive surveillance machine they're secretly building.
—Edward Snowden

We are not alone.

No, we are not referring to aliens and UFOs, but to the eyes and ears that follow us everywhere we go. These eyes and ears belong to humans, and they are tuned in on our actions 24/7 in one way or another.

Privacy and anonymity are things of the past as we enter the brave new world of technology, allowing anyone the opportunity to check in and see what we are doing, who we are with, and where we are—and most of the time we have no clue they are watching us from the shadows. Whether their intention is to see if we are up to no good, or to determine what we buy so we can be sold something else, or just out of sheer curiosity and voyeurism, we no longer control our own personal space, folks. It's up for the taking by anyone with the technological savvy to grab it.

Gone are the days of tapping someone's phone or placing a crude microphone under the desk of a house under surveillance by a P.I. Gone are the days of stealing mail or sitting in a car across the street from a house during a sting operation, eye-balling through a pair of binoculars. Gone are the days of peering through telescopes into the apartment across the way or following someone to keep track of his or her actions.

Now we have satellites, drones, cell phones, and computers to do the dirty work of watching over people, at home or abroad, in their workplaces, and out on the streets.

Electronic Surveillance

Amendment IV

The right of the people to be secure in their persons, houses, papers, and effects, against unreasonable searches and seizures, shall not be violated, and no warrants shall issue, but upon probable cause, supported by oath or affirmation, and particularly describing the place to be searched, and the persons or things to be seized.

The Fourth Amendment to the Constitution lays the foundation for privacy. According to Cornell University's Legal Information Institute Website: "The Fourth Amendment originally enforced the notion that 'each man's home is his castle,' secure from unreasonable searches and seizures of property by the government. It protects against arbitrary arrests, and is the basis of the law regarding search warrants, stop-and-frisk, safety inspections, wiretaps, and other forms of surveillance, as well as being central to many other criminal law topics and to privacy law."

But the advent of electronic surveillance has put our privacy rights in a very precarious position. There are two kinds of electronic surveillance we must contend with—and worry about. Wire communications, which refer simply to those types of communications that involve the transfer of one human voice to another, via cell phone, cable, or some other device, can easily be accessed via an outside source, without the two talking humans ever knowing. Electronic communications refer to the transfer of data, information, or sounds from one location to another location, via a device intended for such transfer. Think computers and e-mail and the Internet and social networking.

Like search and seizures on behalf of the government or law enforcement, electronic surveillance requires a warrant showing probable cause for the invasion of privacy of both parties. Ideally, the reason for concern over a particular conversation, at a particular time, between two particular people must be spelled out in a warrant to make this type of invasive surveillance "legal," and it is far easier for authorities to get away with listening into private conversations when they occur in public places than in someone's home or place of business—but there are ways around all of these legalities.

With the terror attacks of 9/11 and the rise of the Patriot Act shortly after by the George W. Bush administration, surveillance has become the perfectly acceptable, albeit under-the-radar, norm because of these loopholes, where no warrant is required. According to Cornell's Legal Information Institute, some of those instances would include the suspicion of terrorist activity, a threat to a person or institution, suspicions of a conspiracy of organized crime, or suspicion of a threat to national security. The Patriot Act loosened all laws prior to 2001 that made it difficult to wiretap anyone, but especially transmissions that originated in a foreign country or were sent to one. It also got rid of that pesky law that only the president could conduct any "warrantless wiretapping" against any U.S. citizen. This broad sweeping law even allowing for "roving wiretapping," which grants a surveillance warrant without having to name the actual communications carriers. This was deemed necessary to keep an eye on terrorists, who never stayed in one place for long, and applied not just to cell phones, but e-mails as well.

Now while you relax and think that none of those loophole categories apply to you, therefore you are probably never being watched or listened to, think again. These instances can be so broadly applied that even hinting that you hate a particular politician and wish he or she were dead, or telling someone jokingly that you'd love to blow up a particular corporation's headquarters, can get you in a heap of hot water, even under arrest, with your phones, computers, and devices taken from you as "evidence."

Snowden and the NSA

The whole issue of electronic surveillance blew up in 2013 when the *UK Guardian* newspaper released secret documents showing that an American intelligence organization, FISC (Foreign Intelligence Surveillance Court), had demanded the release of daily caller information from one of the biggest cell phone carriers on the planet, Verizon. The person who turned over those documents was Edward Snowden, who worked for the NSA's Oahu office. He began to notice that the NSA was spying on American citizens via cell phone calls and the Internet as part of a clandestine mass electronic data mining surveillance program called PRISM. PRISM was started in 2007 by the NSA after the passage of the Protect America Act, courtesy of then-president George W. Bush, and became the biggest source of raw intelligence data for analysis by U.S. government officials. Even encrypted data could be mined and analyzed under PRISM, which fell under supervision of FISC.

While at the Oahu NSA office, Snowden copied the top-secret documents that he most found disturbing, especially those involving domestic surveillance on millions of average Americans under PRISM. Snowden then asked for a leave of absence, citing illness, and flew to China, where he stayed while the *UK Guardian* published the files he had given them in June 2013. Along with the *Washington Times*, the *Guardian* named the PRISM program and the NSA in the leaked documents, which included even more damning information. Snowden did interviews from his China hotel room, but soon the government stepped in with federal prosecutors charging the whistle-blower with a variety of allegations, including two that fell under the Espionage Act.

The Snowden fallout continued as he went into hiding, with stories surfacing of asylum being offered in different countries. Although he remains in exile as of this writing, Snowden insists he turned over all documents to other journalists, protecting his sources' identities and claiming he did what he did because he felt that the rights of Americans at home and abroad had been violated.

Verizon came under public and media fire, as did AT&T and other carrier services, for turning over public call records even when no evidence existed of any terrorist activity. U.S. telecommunications companies are required by the Communications Assistance for Law Enforcement Act (CALEA) to turn over or intercept communications, so the phone carrier services claimed they were not acting in an illegal capacity, even it if was an unethical one. Snowden stated in an interview with CBS News that he did not think of himself as a hero to the public—just someone who didn't want to live in a world where there was no privacy. Although President Obama tried to calm public fears of spying in January

2014, when he ordered the U.S. attorney general to review the NSA's surveillance programs, the public wasn't buying it. Trust had been broken, and the conspiracy of "Big Brother," which many had insisted and expected existed, was finally exposed for all to see.

There are two kinds of wiretapping involving phones, whether landlines or cellular: Passive wiretapping involves monitoring actual records of call traffic; active wiretapping can alter and change the call traffic. Actual data about a call is a lot easier for a government or law enforcement agency to get a hold of without a warrant, but the call content itself is up for grabs to those who have the means, and the reasons, to access it. What consumers don't seem to understand is that a telephone company has a billing department that keeps *all* data records on file, obviously for the purposes of billing customers appropriately, but this information is available to the right requestors.

An even more frightening situation occurs where personal call recording and interception comes into play. It's one thing to have the CIA or NSA listen to you tell your mom how much your new running shoes were, but the idea that your spouse or significant other, even a stalker, could be listening in—well, that churns the gut. Yet phone conversations can be recorded and monitored by third parties with the right equipment. Remember listening to cordless phone conversations over modified police scanners back in the 1980s and 1990s, before encryption came along and ruined that good-time hobby? Today the technology is more sophisticated and often harder to detect.

When the NSA/Snowden story exploded, many Americans responded on political forums and social networking with the following sentiment: "They can spy on me all they want. I've got nothing to hide. I'm not a Muslim terrorist." Yet what these people didn't seem to know is that the FBI has been monitoring all kinds of people and groups that have nothing to do with Islamic extremism and 9/11–style attacks. In December 2005, the ACLU released information about some of the more chilling targets of FBI monitoring. In "New Documents Show FBI Targeting Environmental and Animal Rights Groups Activities as 'Domestic Terrorism," the ACLU revealed that the FBI was using counterterrorism measures to not only watch, but infiltrate, environmental and animal rights groups including Greenpeace, PETA, and even a community vegan project event at the University of Indiana. Apparently, the FBI thought people who protect animals were terrorists, or as they called them "eco-terrorists," who posed a potential threat against national security.

The ACLU's Ann Beeson, an associate legal director, stated: "Labeling law abiding groups and their members 'domestic terrorists' is not only irresponsible, it has a chilling effect on the vibrant tradition of political dissent in this country."

Beeson hit the nail on the head. Political dissent after 9/11 of *any* kind was looked at as potential terrorism, even lawful protests and non-violent civil disobedience. Suddenly, anyone who ever contributed to PETA or attended a Greenpeace protest was considered a threat to national security. One has to wonder why the feds chose these groups to focus on when there were ample numbers of domestic terrorist groups causing racial violence, and even murder, across the nation.

Heck, even the Catholic Workers Group (CWG) was put under surveillance for possible "Communist leanings." In truth, the CWG proposed peace and the sharing of resources, something the FBI deemed "Communistic." Even poverty relief groups and labor unions were put under the Fed's microscope, causing an outcry among civil rights advocates over the Bush administration's blurred lines between actual terrorist activity, and lawful protests, including civil disobedience.

After 9/11, Americans were screaming for more protection from the "bad guys," never realizing that they themselves might end up on the "bad guy" list one day.

Elana Freeland writes in "This Covert Electromagnetic Era" that 9/11 was indeed a dramatic turning point in many ways:

> ...One being the increased use of electromagnetic weapons for public shock and awe—from electronic surveillance technology like radiating devices and receivers, non-radiating devices, and laser-facilitated listening devices, both ground and satellite, to "hot on the hook" phones, "smart phones," eXaudio software to detect and decode emotions.... Remotely controlled open source data surveillance technology like computers, pattern recognition, voice- and thought-activation, including brain wave monitoring of thoughts, is now big business. (Thus the term military-*industrial* complex.) In this unseen electromagnetic era,

the line between military and civilian is radically disappearing as the military redefines all of life as a "battlespace."

Chilling words—and what irony that after the terrorist attacks of 9/11, our own government took our civil liberties hostage. Who needs the foreign terrorists with friends like that?

Cyber Spies

In August 2013, *Mother Jones Magazine* published an article titled "How to Keep the NSA Out of Your Computer." Written by *Wired* columnist Clive Thompson, the article detailed an actual method for keeping those pesky feds off your cyberspace, by utilizing a "private, parallel Internet" other than the one that requires you to pay a service provider a fee to get online. This private Internet is achieved by building a link of Wi-Fi antennae that create a literal "mesh" that can pass along data and signals much faster than the ordinary Net speed we pay for. The mesh concept originated in Athens, Greece, and proved to be a reliable means of creating a "roll your own" network for a community to use, and stay under the radar of the snooping NSA and friends. All it required was some free equipment, and more than 1,000 Athenians were up and running a network that can be built anywhere.

Thompson says the Mesh resembles a community food co-op, with members setting up their own equipment to allow their computer's Wi-Fi hubs to pass along the signal to anyone else with the equipment in their vicinity. One hub at a time. In Spain, the Guifi Mesh network grew into the world's largest, with more than 21,000 members. Isaac Wilder, cofounder of the Free Network Foundation, is using this Mesh model to wire up neighborhoods with low incomes, which cannot afford the typical Internet service fees. Mesh systems were created to provide an economic benefit, but they also have the added benefit of allowing political activism a safer, more reliable method of communications that is not beholden to the big IP providers and government oversight.

"The notion of a truly independent global Internet may still be a gleam in the eye of the Meshers, but their visionary zeal is contagious," Thompson writes.

So your cell phone might be the culprit but, rest assured, cyber-spying works just as well. Maybe even better. Web-tapping logs the IP address of a user that accesses certain Websites, and allows a third party to easily monitor any and all sites visited. Again, permitted by the Patriot Act, your searches and browser history may be set to private, but that only protects you from being busted by someone in your own household.

It does not protect you from the federal agents who are concerned with your penchant for Googling certain key terms that strike up a red flag in the "terrorist term data base." You could even get nailed for child porn charges if you accidentally stumble on certain sites in your search for a little afternoon cyber-delight.

Speaking of Google, the NSA has its own Google-style search engine called ICREACH, according to the documents released by Snowden, that is built to share more than 850 billion records of phone calls, e-mails, cell phone locations, faxes, private messages and chats, and social networking posts. ICREACH is meant to pinpoint information on the private communications of foreigners, but it cannot avoid also exposing the private messages of millions of American citizens who have nothing to do with potential terrorist activities. ICREACH is allegedly accessible, according to "The Surveillance Engine: How the NSA Built Its Own Secret Google" for FirstLook.org's "The Intercept," to thousands of U.S. government agency analysts involving intelligence work for the DEA, FBI, CIA, DIA, and others. It was specifically designed to be the largest internal database of secret surveillance records in the United States, with the capability of handling up to five billion new records each day.

Legal experts were shocked at the sheer magnitude of ICREACH's reach. Elizabeth Goitein, co-director of the Liberty and National Security Program at the New York University School of Law stated, "To me, this is extremely troublesome. The myth that metadata is just a bunch of numbers and is not as revealing as actual communications content was exploded long ago—this is a trove of incredibly sensitive information."

Sadly for the folks in merry old England, the director general of the Office for Security and Counter-Terrorism, Charles Farr, stated that the surveillance of such popular Websites as Google, Twitter, YouTube, and Facebook by government agencies was perfectly legal by redefining them as "external communications." This allows a range of activities from chats to e-mails to postings to be fair game for indiscriminate data collection and analysis.

Automated Internet surveillance of any kind looks for particular search and key words and phrases that might be associated with any kind of domestic or foreign terrorism, criminal activity, child porn, or threats to national security. The sheer amount of data that must be searched is mind-boggling, thus relying on actual computers themselves to sift through the information looking for trigger words. This includes e-mails (stored in a massive NSA database called Pinwale) and private messaging, chats, and social networking. If it can be typed into a computer, it can be searched. Not to mention that data remains stored on personal computers, making it easy to access anytime. The FBI even has its own software that can be installed on a computer system in person or remotely to keep track of keystrokes and search terms.

Data from social networking sites provides a whole new arena for snooping on potential spies, whistle-blowers, terrorists, and rebel-rousers, with traffic analysis maps created from mined data. This data might reveal affiliations with known terrorists and terrorist groups, potential violent activity, even beliefs and ideologies considered dangerous to U.S. interests here and abroad. Be careful what you post, people!

Cyber stalking and bullying prove how easy it is to find out who is where and doing what, and to also use that information against someone—possibly to the point of driving them to suicide. Though the government's surveillance may be more about finding bad guys in a sea of data than it is about pushing people around, there is no doubt the opportunity for anyone getting into your computer to do some dirty work (deleting files, adding searches you've never yourself done) to incriminate you in some future crime.

In "Big Brother Is Coming," Salon.com reporters Catherine Crump and Matthew Hardwood suggest that we worry about living our entire lives online by the year 2020, when there could be more than 30 billion devices connected to the Internet. Called "Big Data," this technological "Big Brother" will control our household appliances, our cars, and even the lights in our parking garages, among other things. Everything we do will be done via the Internet. "A future Internet of Things does have the potential to offer real benefits," the writers state, "but the dark side of that seemingly shiny coin is this: companies will increasingly know all there is to know about you." The writers continue: "In the not-too-distant future, however, real space will be increasingly like cyberspace... with the rise of the networked device, what people do in their homes, in their cars, in stores, and within their communities will be monitored and analyzed in ever more intrusive ways by corporations and, by extension, the government."

Smart homes are being built where even smoke detectors and fire alarms are linked to the Net, and have the "intelligence" to discern between a real fire and burnt toast. Smart TV can turn on and tune in to our favorite channel before we even get home from work. Smart fridges can get the beer ready. Smart garages will open the door when you're a mile down the road. Go to a local restaurant and already apps like iBeacon and Turnstyle on your Smartphone track your location and can even turn on a microphone in your phone to listen in on your conversations. Turnstyle Solutions even has sensors around the city of Toronto, Canada, that can track your every movement—and if you log onto Facebook, even better, for the Wi-Fi network you might be using was in fact installed by Turnstyle itself and now has access to all of your social networking identity and data.

Go outside and you will find smart streetlamps made with energy efficient LEDs, like the lights found at Newark Liberty International Airport. Interestingly, these lights also double as surveillance cameras and sensors used by the Port Authority to monitor long lines, identify license plates on cars, and watch for suspicious activity around the airport. Speaking of license plates, there already exists an infrastructure of cameras that take pictures of passing cars in order to help identify drivers for law enforcement purposes. Chances are, your car is in the photo album!

The smart technology can do it all, but are we being dumb for giving up control of our lives to the Internet, and the watchful eyes behind it?

Commercial Mass Surveillance

Commercial mass surveillance takes advantage of the massive amounts of stored data via cell phones and computers, and uses it to gather information about what people spend money on, what they do for fun, where they like to shop or vacation, and a host of other questions that could result in bigger profits for corporations behind the spy games. One of the less-sinister ways this is done is via "store cards" or reward cards offered by various grocery stores or shopping outlets that allow a person to sign up via the internet or a phone app, and—voila!—their shopping habits are documented for the corporate headquarters to see and analyze. The benefits to the consumer are better prices and special deals and offers, but often at the loss of even more of their precious remaining privacy.

Like Google AdSense and OpenSocial and Facebook Ads, the Internet also employs this commercial type of social programming, trolling for useable data among user profiles and posts, and looking for marketing trends and shifts that can be taken advantage of. Mobile and location tracking services that "geolocate" the user add an even greater amount of data that can be used to glean preferences in shopping, dining, and entertainment, even if it's at the cost of the user's privacy. If the user is engaging a mobile geolocator or some type of location-based advertising service, including those that allow you to search for nearby eateries and clubs, then the user is pretty much a live target for physical tracking, as she is revealing her whereabouts each time she checks in.

Basically, in our quest to embrace faster, better, and more, at least when it comes to technology, we have given up our rights to privacy in so many ways to prying eyes, and yet so few people have given up their cell phones or computers. Therefore, the threat of a police state, or surveillance state, where the masses are under watchful control by authority entities from the government, military, and even big business, appears to be a threat that is readily acceptable over the horrifying thought of giving up our gadgets.

Eyes in the Sky

Look around any city street and you are likely to see a surveillance camera on a pole peering down at you. In stores and office buildings, airports and convention centers, restaurants and warehouses, surveillance cameras watch your every move, looking for suspicious behaviors and actions. Once the domain of law enforcement for taking a bite out of crime, cameras are now often part of Homeland Security's quest to root out potential bad guys/terrorists, using a web of cameras that report back to a central monitoring system that may or may not be operated by actual human beings. Surveillance has, like everything else, gone digital, with actual data now going into large databases to be analyzed by special computer software that looks for specific parameters, depending on the agency behind the surveillance and the location of the cameras.

Whether on the streets to watch foot traffic, or installed at intersections to monitor traffic violations, or at a major sports event to keep track of potential fights and riots, camera surveillance is rampant and often right under our noses, or above our noses, and rarely do we bother to look up and take notice. Most people expect to be under the scrutiny of security cameras when they walk into a DMV or government office, or the halls of academia, or the headquarters of a swanky corporation, but the proliferation of spying devices that track our every move is mind-boggling, and one day may be on every street corner of every city in the nation. Why? We can blame the Patriot Act and the growing paranoia of the public for that. We wanted more security, and we got it, with Homeland Security behind a push for greater surveillance that leads back to their central monitoring center where they can then peer at the images, via databases that even have face recognition capabilities, which determine if a potential threat exists.

In the mid-2000s, after the 9/11 threats created a strong sense of paranoia and fear in urban centers, Mayor Richard Daley ordered a program called Operation Virtual Shield (OVS) for the city of Chicago. OVS consisted of thousands of surveillance cameras that linked to a central monitoring system that captured raw video footage in real time. The program cost more than $200 million to implement, paid for by the Department of Homeland Security, and allowed city officials and law enforcement to literally expand the use of cameras, as well as biological, chemical, and radiological sensors that would all feed into the city's Operations Center, where they could be monitored by officials, including the Office of Emergency Services, for potential criminal activity, terrorism, and even disaster response.

In 2014, the ACLU stepped in to speak out against the use of surveillance cameras in the city of St. Louis, Missouri, citing the lack of central guidelines and reporting of the data of the surveillance network, not to mention a lack of public disclosure about the program. Over the past two years, the city of St. Louis had expanded its surveillance ability with more cameras, and four linked surveillance networks that fed into a central monitoring center at the Soldiers Memorial. But the ACLU, under executive director Jeffrey Mittman, warned of becoming a surveillance society, even as the city's mayor's office was praising the new system as a means of making the public safer.

On a much larger scale, DARPA developed the program Combat Eyes That See, or CTS, in conjunction with the Pentagon, to become the widest reaching and most invasive surveillance system in the United States. CTS, developed by several major corporations and universities, was designed to also be used oversees to protect our troops in combat zones, which sounds like a good idea, but red flags arose when the program looked like it would also be used on American soil, using face recognition and license plate imaging, among other methods, to keep an eye on entire cities and their citizens. In "Big Brother Gets a Brain," for the July 8, 2003, *Village Voice* issue, reporter Noah Shachtman wrote, "Make a move considered suspicious and CTS will instantly report you to the authorities."

Although begun as a military program to try and stop terrorist activity before it happens, some see CTS as the future, where Big Brother watches over us all from one central, all-seeing eye, and the scary thing is, what we may think of as normal behavior could be interpreted as suspicious activity.

Ohio-based company Persistent Surveillance Systems (PSS) hopes that one day every city in the country will use its high-tech cameras to reduce crime. PSS uses a camera mounted on a Cessna aircraft, called the Hawk Eye II, for some of its missions, and president Ross McNutt claims it can spot as many as 50 crimes per six-hour flight, according to an interview with Ty Wright for the *Washington Post*'s Business and Technology Feb. 2014 edition. McNutt sees PSS as not just a means for reducing crime, but also bring "substantial side effects, including rising property values, better schools, increased development and, eventually, lower incarceration rates as the reality of long-term overhead surveillance deters those tempted to commit crimes."

Here is a perfect example of a corporate interest aligning with law enforcement, as the support and acceptance of PSS by many police agencies promises bigger profits for PSS. Never mind that, there is no guarantee that PSS won't be watching people who are *not* about to commit a crime, whether by accident or on purpose, as part of its quest to create an overhead spy system that is capable of streaming images continuously across a five mile by five-mile area.

Right now, the technology of PSS is limited and lacks the ability to hone in on a person and tell what color underwear he is wearing. But McNutt promises that he intends to increase the range so larger areas can be covered. But planes can also carry infrared sensors that can track people, vehicles, even wildlife at night "even through some foliage and into some structures, such as tents." McNutt will no doubt increase the precision and resolution of imagery as well. Make sure you are wearing your clean undies, folks.

Never has our privacy been invaded more insidiously. Well, then again...

Space Spies

Look a little higher into the sky and there are more eyes watching, from satellites orbiting the planet, fighting crime from outer space. Highly sensitive surveillance imaging from satellites is helping to spot criminals, find dead bodies, locate terrorists and their hideouts, and even spot large-scale illegal waste disposal, among other things. Big Brother isn't just global anymore.

Satellite technology has increased to the point where a small object can be pinpointed from space, not to mention your car in your driveway or that ugly garden gnome in your backyard. The cost effectiveness of space surveillance and the ability to identify targets with increasing high resolution are making this the industry standard, according to Patricia Lewis, research director of International Security at the think tank Chatham House. Lewis believes that these satellite systems will be used not just by law enforcement but also by anyone working in international security. "Drug trafficking and arms reduction treaties are among the priority applications," Lewis said in an interview with Kieron Monks for CNNTech's "Spy Satellites Fight Crime From Space." However, as resolution increases to the point of being able to identify a person's face, ethical questions involving privacy rights will come into play.

In the June 19, 2003, article "The Menace of Satellite Surveillance" on EducateYourself.org, author/researcher John Flemming makes a chilling opening statement: "A spy satellite can monitor a person's every movement, even when the 'target' is indoors or deep in the interior of a building or traveling rapidly down the highway in a car, in any kind of weather.... There is no place to hide on the face of the earth."

According to Flemming, it only takes three satellites to watch over the entire planet with detection capacity, relaying data back to computers on earth that then look for specific activity. One only has to look at the main powerhouses behind this kind of surveillance—government and intelligence agencies, including defense and military, as well as defense-related corporations like Lockheed and Boeing—to suppose the main motives for global spying from above. Though spy satellites have been around for decades (remember President Reagan's proposed "Star Wars" initiative back in the early 1980s?), the amazing progress of technology has made it more invasive, with the capacity to watch over more and more individuals at any given time. Flemming warns of the links between satellite surveillance and technologies that peer into the brain, looking for the genesis of thoughts and emotions, and "read a person's mind from space."

Though the chances still remain small that any one individual in particular is being watched from space at any given time, and if an individual is not part of a terrorist group or has no known reason to be watched in the first place, there is still the creepy sense of someone always overhead that *can* watch you, if desired, and the future holds even more promise of those chances increasing. Right now, though, there are smaller objects closer to home that can spy through your windows, or walls, or follow you down alleys and through the woods to Grandmother's house (or anywhere else you plan to go).

Drone Nation

Drone surveillance is the new kid on the block, used by government agencies and law enforcement as the new "unmanned police state" mode of keeping the public safe. The growing use of small, remote controlled drones for both commercial and security purposes is in the news all the time, yet few people seem outraged by the flying bugs in the sky, except when we learn of one being utilized in war. (Yes, they fight wars, too!)

But think about this: More and more police departments in major urban centers are using drones to keep criminals under watch, and the FAA estimated that by the year 2020 there will be more than 7,000 civilian drones in the sky, not to mention the many that will be flying without any oversight. In fact, there exists no legal governing laws right now to regulate the use of drones, meaning that whoever desires to put one in the sky can do so, including law enforcement agencies that can convince their citizens of the benefits to public safety. But drone resistance is growing, even as more are spotted in the skies, with the National Conference of State Legislatures reporting more than 70 bills from 40 states concerning the use of drones.

Domestic drone use is creating a new kind of routine aerial surveillance that makes the public extra nervous, yet has also created a new kind of rebellion, with people taking it upon themselves to shoot down the metal birds in the sky. And speaking of birds, recent news reports across the country reported that birds, especially larger birds of prey, were knocking drones out of the sky, seeing them as "foreign threats" of their territory!

Because drones are so much more visible than surveillance satellites and hidden cameras, one has to wonder how pervasive a privacy threat they will become. But for use in warfare and on battlefields, and for going into dangerous crime-ridden areas or geographical regions that would be difficult for ground troops or police, they can indeed be a blessing. Drones used overseas in warfare are indeed equipped with weapons technology, something that state legislatures demand should be prohibited for domestic drone use. Demands also include only allowing drone usage during riots or emergencies, in which case they can help identify trouble spots and collect evidence.

One of the biggest problems with the use of drones is knowing that terrorists can use them, too. In October 2014, several instances of unmanned drones flying over France's state-owned nuclear power plant were reported in the news. Fly-bys were reported by the Creys-Malville power plant, as well as other locations throughout southeast France, mostly at night and in the early morning

A MQ-9 Reaper unmanned aerial drone on a mission during Operation Enduring Freedom in Afghanistan, 2007. USAF image from USAF Photographic Archives.

hours. Though the French Air Force tried to play down the threat by describing the small drones as commercial and therefore too small to be a problem, groups like Greenpeace questioned that approach, accusing the French leaders of minimizing a serious threat of unknown drones that could have been weapons-equipped.

In New York City, the NYPD voiced active concerns about drones in the hands of terrorists as a very clear and present danger. Talking to CBS News reporter Jeff Pegues, the NYPD had no intelligence showing an imminent threat, but worried that drones might be used in a potential future attack. Deputy Police Chief Salvatore DiPace was quoted as saying, "We look at it as something that could be a terrorist's tool." And why not—because small drones are controlled remotely, can be equipped with weapons including poison gasses and germ warfare, and can move around somewhat undetected until they do their dirty deed. NYPD officials were indeed worried, especially after two of their Aviation Unit members, Officer Daryl Maudsley and Sergeant Antonio Hernandez, came face to face with an unidentified drone—while they were flying their helicopter at night! "We're flying in the dark, we have night-vision goggles on, we're trying to get a job done and then the next thing you know we see this drone come up to our altitude," Hernandez said.

The two men had no idea who the drone belonged to and what it was capable of. "You don't know what the intentions are...hostile, recreational; there's a lot of different ways you can go with that," Maudsley said.

Hobbyists have discovered the world of drone building, and anyone can buy a kit for anywhere from a few hundred to a few thousand dollars, depending on the capabilities. Building and flying remote controlled drones has even spawned clubs across the country, and one has to ask: How might we tell the difference between a law enforcement drone spying on us, and the creepy guy down the block using one to see us undressing at night? Maybe stories of civilians shooting down drones will become the norm.

This year, in 2015, the FAA has introduced a proposal for new drone operating regulations that could open the airways to over 7,000 new private companies that wish to operate their own drones. The proposal could also make it easier for drones to be operated outside of the pilot's line of site (critical for delivery purposes), open up government transparency of drone use, and also require a basic certification for users operating drones for a private company. These new regulations, if approved, are likely to expand into more rules that allow even more drones in the skies as pressure is put upon the FAA by corporate, private, law enforcement, government, and military entities who see the benefits of going drone-ward. For us civilians down here on the ground, there are benefits to be sure, but also fears and concerns of a sky filled with little prying eyes and ears...or even worse, weapons.

It's just hard to look up, see a little remote controlled device hovering outside your window, and not feel the urge to blast the sucker out of the heavens—something no doubt tempting to those who feel their land is being trespassed on and their privacy rights trampled on. And with drones that take images as they hover, it creates a deeper sense of paranoia and fear for a public already inundated with technologies that are spying on them. Remote controlled planes are a thing of the past. Drones are here and coming soon to hover in a neighborhood near you.

Chipped Off!

One of the most insidious forms of control and surveillance really gets under your skin—literally. Conspiracy theorists have long been

A collection of commercially used RFID tags. Wikipedia image made available under the GNU Free Documentation license.

talking of the day when humans are chipped, like animals at the pound. These microchips will not only include all of our genetic data, but our medical records, banking history, and employment records. Our very identity will come down to a tiny chip implanted somewhere under our skin, possibly even against our will or without our knowledge. The chip will also enable someone to track our whereabouts via remote devices.

Welcome to the world of radio frequency identification (RFID) tags, which are tiny wireless smart bar codes that are hooked up to electronic readers that can track and identify things like the food and products we buy at a grocery store. Tame enough, right? RFID tags are already in use to track vehicles, pets, and even people with illnesses like Alzheimer's. The tags contain electronically stored information that is sent over a particular radio frequency to a data capture location, and come in handy for companies that want to track their products as they are made and shipped. Even livestock get chipped.

But privacy concerns arise when people-implanted chips with personal information included in the tags can get into the "wrong" hands. RFIDs can be passive, active, or battery-assisted/passive. Passive RFIDs have no batteries and are considered less desirable than active and battery-assisted versions, which include the ability to transmit ID signals to an RFID reader without much interference. There are two types of readers as well: Active Reader Passive Tag systems, which transmit encoded radio signals to "interrogate" or read a tag, as well as receive authentication replies from passive tags; and Active Reader Active Tags, which interface with active tags from active readers, and work with battery-assisted passive tags as well. Confusing, but rest assured, the right RFID can scan and transmit the right information depending on the motives of the company using the chips, and what they want and need the information for. They are basically two-way radio transmitters/receivers of data that can be implanted in anything to keep track of its location.

RFIDs simply use different bandwidths of the radio wave spectrum to signal and transmit over, and may or may not require close proximity to reader antennae. Privacy issues arise over the sheer fact that these tiny objects are implanted into things and we don't often know they are, and they transmit information and data about our credit card, store card, and shopping and consumer behaviors and actions, not to mention our identities and bank information. Not to mention the fact that the RFIDs continue to transmit data once the product purchased is taken home, which suggests the possibility of surveillance that is not related to consumer usage. Special concern is given to store cards and credit cards that are chipped, which continuously may be transmitting information or being tracked from an external source. (There is a way around this, folks. Cover the card with aluminum foil!)

But the biggest threat comes from the possibility of human use. Could the government one day force people to be implanted with a chip, or deny them the right to buy products and services? Could the Big Brothers out there demand that this method of human identification become the norm, and dole out punishment to those who refuse to be marked? Could you be tagged during your next hospital visit, while out cold from anesthesia, and not be informed? Could you already be tagged and not even know that somebody out there knows your every move and/or your every action?

It's one thing to tag a part for a tractor so that the company can watch its progress through the assembly line, but another entirely for a person to be forced to have his entire medical history, financial and educational backgrounds, and other identifying markers implanted under his skin as part of a national ID system to have access to any type of data at any time without the person feeling or knowing a thing.

Big Brother is watching, all the time, from every angle possible. The question is: How much more of our precious privacy will we give away for the sake of safety, security, and the profits of huge corporations that want to know what we buy and use? Although we may indeed be under some form of surveillance at any given time, we can still raise a middle finger to those peering, prying eyes by becoming aware of the capabilities of modern surveillance technology—and who is behind the curtain using it to spy on us.

CONCLUSION:
WHO OWNS YOUR MIND?

The trouble with having an open mind, of course, is that people will insist on coming along and trying to put things in it.
—Terry Pratchett

Relying on the government to protect your privacy is like asking a peeping tom to install your window blinds.
—John Perry Barlow

Dr. Michael Persinger, whom we have written about in previous books, is a professor of psychology and neuroscience at Ontario, Canada's Laurentian University, and a well-respected scientist. His work with electromagnetic fields and their influences on the human brain includes the use of temporal lobe stimulation to invoke the sensation of being watched, seeing "paranormal" shadow entities, experiencing perceptual anomalies, even causing nightmares. But it was his article "On the Possibility of Directly Accessing Every Human Brain by Electromagnetic Induction of Fundamental Algorithms" that set the mind control world on fire. Published in 1995 for *Perceptual and Motor Skills*, the article then appeared (and still does) on a number of science and conspiracy Websites.

Persinger's article foretold of a stunning potential achievement that suggested that there existed these fundamental algorithms by which sensory transduction could be generated into intrinsic, brain specific-code, according to the article's abstract. This code could then be used in direct stimulation of the temporal or limbic cortices by applied electromagnetic patterns requiring energy levels "which are within the range of both geomagnetic activity and contemporary communications networks." He went on to write that this process could be coupled to the narrow band of brain temperatures, allowing "all normal human brains to be affected by a sub-harmonic whose frequency range at about 10 Hz would vary only by 1.0 Hz."

Persinger understood that the last few decades of research into neuroscience, coupled with advancements in technology, were leading to, as he put it, "a potential" that was marginally feasible at the time. That potential? "[T]he technical capability to influence directly the major portion of the approximately six billion brains of the human species, without mediation through classical sensory modalities, by generating neural information within a physical medium within which all members of the species are immersed."

The Matrix, anyone?

Now you can read and reread that over and over again, but the implication will remain the same: We are on the verge, if we haven't already succeeded, of creating technologies that can *control the minds of the masses on a global scale*. Whether this control comes in the form of neural programming designed to change our beliefs and behaviors, or some form of "mass consciousness manipulation," the potential is there for both positive and more nefarious purposes. People in the scientific field, no doubt being urged on by governments and military organizations and corporations, are looking for ways to make our minds up for us.

The question is: Do we have a choice in the matter?

Two news stories present a chilling look into the brave, new world we face. One, "Mind Control Scientists Claim Ability to Turn Off Consciousness," reported by Nick West for *The Sleuth Journal* in July 2014, looks at the cutting-edge BRAIN project in the United States, and the British counterpart, the HUMAN BRAIN PROJECT, which will examine the possibility of brain-computer interfacing, the implanting and erasure of memories, and even the direct uploading of information to the brain. But even more shocking is the claim of George Washington University scientists, published in the *Epilepsy and Behavior Journal*, and reported by *New Scientist*'s Helen Thomson in her July 2014 article,

"Consciousness On-off Switch Discovered Deep in Brain." Led by neuroscientist Mohamad Koubeissi, the team of scientists switched off and on the consciousness of a woman subject by stimulating her claustrum (a thin sheet of neurons attached to the underside of the neocortex in the center of the brain). The subject suffered from epilepsy and had hooked her brain up with electrodes, one of which was close to the claustrum, an area never before stimulated in any studies.

The result, when zapped with high-frequency electrical impulses, was a loss of consciousness. When the stimulation stopped, she immediately regained consciousness and couldn't remember anything before that moment of having lost consciousness!

The second story, "Neuroscience Could Mean Soldiers Controlling Weapons With Minds," for the *UK Guardian*'s February 2012 edition, looks at cutting-edge research to create a better soldier by having their minds plugged directly into their weapons. The original report was published in the UK National Academy of Science's Royal Society Report, and also claimed that future research might lead to drugs that can boost soldier performance, get captives and enemies to talk, and make enemy troops fall asleep. All of this would be achieved by passing weak electrical signals through the skull using transcranial direct current stimulation (tDCS). V2K anyone?

Our brains, our minds, and even our consciousness may no longer be a privately owned and operated domain.

Back in 1975, the United Nations General Assembly considered a draft proposed by the then–Soviet Union titled "Prohibition of the Development and Manufacture of New Types of Weapons of Mass Destruction and New Systems of Such Weapons." Among some of the later weapons systems listed were:

1. Radiological weapons that could produce effects similar to those of a nuclear explosion.
2. Particle beam weapons using charged or neutral particles to affect biological targets.
3. Infrasonic acoustic radiation weapons.
4. Electromagnetic weapons operating at certain radio-frequency radiations, which would have injurious effects on human organs.

Unfortunately, the response from Western nations was no response.

Other treaties, such as biological and chemical weapons bans (both on the battlefield and in the city streets), have been created and modified, but apparently, not one that stops the invasion of the human mind, or the use of mediums such as microwaves or infrasound for individual harassment. And, the push for non-lethal weapons, especially for use by law enforcement against civilians, gives the appearance of a "kindler, gentler" assault on freedoms and liberties. Perhaps a number of authoritative entities agree not to nuke each other, but nothing stops them from using the cutting-edge technology of the times to invade, alter, and manipulate human emotions, thoughts, behaviors, and actions. At least they aren't killing anyone, right?

According to Judy Wall, editor and publisher of *Resonance: The Bioelectromagnetic Special Interest Group*, in an article titled "Military Use of Silent Sound: Mind Control Weapons," psy-ops (psychological weaponry) was used in the Persian Gulf War. The technology utilized consisted of "subliminal, mind-altering technology...carried on standard radiofrequency broadcasts." There were even news briefs in March 1991 stating that the use of psy-ops had occurred once Saddam Hussein's military command-and-control system was destroyed. "High-Tech Psychological Warfare Arrives in the Middle East," a news brief, described a psy-ops used against the Iraqi troops during Operation Desert Storm in which U.S. transmitters overpowered local Iraqi stations and began broadcasting patriotic and religious music, along with "vague, confusing and contradictory military orders and information." Wall writes that this may have also included a more powerful, subliminal technology at work that used "a sophisticated electronic system to 'speak' directly to the mind of the listener, to alter and entrain his brainwaves, to manipulate his brain's electroencephalograph, i.e. EEG patterns and artificially implant negative emotional states-feelings of fear, anxiety, despair and hopelessness."

Perhaps that is why, as Wall states, Iraqi troops later surrendered en masse, including majors and brigade commanders who gave up their entire units. What messages might have been coursing through the brains of these soldiers, who at one point fought for their beliefs, and then reversed and gave up?

Well, in 1992, Dr. Oliver Lowery of Norcross, Georgia, developed the "Silent Subliminal Presentation System," that stated "modulated carriers may be transmitted directly in real time, or may be conveniently recorded and stored on mechanical, magnetic or optical media for delayed or repeated transmission to the listener." Hell, now you could not only beam a message into the brain once, you could store that message and have it beamed repeatedly! Edward Tilton, president of a company called Silent Sounds, Inc., calls this technology "S-quad" and allegedly stated in a letter dated December 13, 1996, according to Judy Wall for *Nexus Magazine*, that they could "use supercomputers to analyze human emotional EEG patterns and replicate them, then store these 'emotion signature clusters' on another computer, and, at will, 'silently induce and change the emotional state in a human being.'" Interestingly, Silent Sounds, Inc. stated its schematics were classified by the U.S. government, used by the German government and even the Soviets, and—get this— "The system was used throughout Operation Desert Storm (Iraq) quite successfully."

Okay, so we are trying to drive home a point here. If these technologies existed back in the 1990s, and we did nothing to stop them, what are we facing now? Is technology too far gone? Have those who wish to control us already won? We are now decades ahead and dealing with modalities that were probably unimaginable 25 years ago. Things have changed. Why anyone would deny this stuff exists is getting a little old.

We live in the age of hovering drones of every size, cameras on every cell phone and street corner, tracking devices we don't even know we are carrying, mass media and the Internet and social networking invading our every waking moment with other people's agendas and ideas of what we should be doing and thinking, and technologies that are so insidious and invisible we probably have no clue we are under assault in the first place. We are stalked, followed, tracked, harassed, pushed, pulled, manipulated, changed, controlled, altered, fooled, ripped off, and deceived in every manner possible, and plenty we probably thought were impossible.

Our bodies and our minds no longer seem to belong to us.

Love music? Even music has been used as a means of behavior modification, if not downright torture. Psy-ops involving blasting loud or obnoxious music sounds like a bad joke, but not to those who have been exposed to this rather invasive assault on the senses. Even though the United Nations and the European Court of Human Rights have banned this form of torture, it was used on prisoners of war in the notorious Abu Ghraib and Guantanamo containment facilities, as well as to flush out the followers of David Koresh in Waco, Texas, and even back in December 1989 when music was used to flush out Manuel Noriega from Holy See's embassy during the U.S. invasion of Panama.

Music, it seems, has the ability to not just incapacitate the mind, but to control it as well. An October 2012 *Scientific American* article titled "The Power of Music" looks at the use of rhythmic sound patterns on the brain and the ability to affect deeper mental processes with such bad back beats. Music has been proven to tap into the brain's emotional center, but also the circuitry involving bodily movement, and can actually control both the emotions and movement. According to the article, at a meeting of the Society for Neuroscience, psychologist Annett Schirmer reported that rhythmic sound "not only coordinates the behavior of people in a group, it also coordinates their thinking—the mental processes of individuals in the group become synchronized." This explains why rituals involving music often put people into trances, and trance dancing and raves are as good as drugs to alter consciousness. It also explains the power of drumming, chanting, and repetitive tribal beats to move people on such a deep, primal level.

Chillingly, it could also explain why people get violent at particular concerts or display more aggression at a heavy metal or punk concert than they would at a performance by a string quartet. Music changes us, and it moves us—but now it seems, it can also control our minds and thoughts, even in a group setting. Is it only a matter of time before we are all behaving like the Walking Dead, zombified by music piped into our homes via the many means of technology at our disposal? Not everyone sees this as a negative, though. Schirmer herself states at the end of the previously mentioned article: "When people move in synchrony they are more likely to perceive the world in synchrony, so that would facilitate their ability to interact."

That perception, and interaction, could go either way: for good or for evil.

But because we have hope, we authors did not want to end this book on such a dark, paranoid, and negatively hopeless and despairing note. Though indeed we are experiencing all forms of mind control and electronic assaults, we still have individual will and resourcefulness, not to mention a stubborn streak that makes us human. In order to retain our humanity, our freedom, and our individuality, we must not stick our heads in the sand as to what occurred in our past, what is happening now, and what might be coming down the pike.

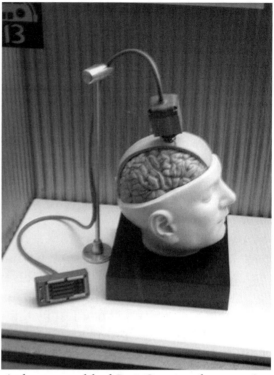

A dummy model of BrainGate interface at a Star Wars exhibition of the Boston Science Museum, 2006. Image by Paul Wicks.

Knowledge is power. Awareness is power. Understanding is power.

Remember, too, that controlling the mind can be a good thing, in terms of achieving goals. If the self-help movement has taught us anything, the power of the mind to create our realities is something to celebrate, not to fear. The use of affirmations, goal-setting techniques, intention, focused thought, and even hypnosis has helped many a person lose weight, stop smoking, get healthy, meet a mate, and succeed at achieving a dream. It isn't all bad when we talk about mind control, as long as we are the ones in control of our own minds—and thus our thoughts, intentions, focus, behaviors, actions, and destinies.

In fact, the same technology discussed earlier, which can influence the brain, might also be used one day to help us live better lives. The concept of "brain hacking," or using implanted chips in the brain to deliver electrical impulses that could help us remember more, focus better, and achieve more goals is not so far-fetched. Gary Marcus, professor of psychology at New York University, and editor of the book *The Future of the Brain: Essays by the World's Leading Neuroscientists*, told Yahoo. com Business Insider in August 2014 that we are on the verge of understanding the brain, even decoding it. We are already sending sound pulses into the brains of the deaf to enable them to hear. We are already using electrical stimulation to study and one day treat depression and other mental illnesses.

Perhaps having a chip in our brains that sends out specific electrical charges that are designed specifically to cure what ails us might literally serve to supercharge the brain.

We might even be able to move stuff around with our brain's own electrical impulses in what is being called *brain–computer interfacing*. In 2011, researchers at Brown University successfully tested the "BrainGate," a type of brain–computer interface that allowed a paralyzed woman to move a cursor just by thinking about it. This opens the door to not just neural prosthetics, but chips that can help us work with computers in a whole new and rather intimate way. We could, one day, be able to tap into a computer's memory banks and fill our brains with all kinds of information. Though this sounds like a great idea on the surface, the possibility for misuse exists. Who designs the chips? Can we be sure they are not going to control our brains even as they expand them? What kind of data will we be accessing, and who controls the flow of that data? How will our brains know to filter out the bad data from the good?

We may be facing questions we cannot answer and making choices that we don't have all of the ramifications for. The problems in life arise when one of two things happens. We either don't control our own minds, thus allowing others to take control—or we do control our own minds, but not with information, wisdom, and knowledge that empower us. Just having a mind doesn't automatically lead to joy, happiness, health, and success. It has to be used right. Remember: A mind is a terrible thing to waste, or to turn over to other forces that most likely do not have our highest good in mind.

Although this book may have only scratched the surface of the history of the more spooky aspects of mind control, social programming, electronic harassment, surveillance, and spying, we hope it has opened your eyes and your mind enough to want to know more, and to read and learn more, about this frightening aspect of our human existence. The rabbit hole goes much deeper than this, and it is all too easy to get sucked down into those dark and eerie depths, and feel as though you can never climb back out.

What is real and what is the realm of pure conspiracy? What is the truth that usually exists in between? And what can we do about it anyway, because don't the powers that are behind these technologies and agendas have the ability to keep us from doing anything about it?

Only if we let them.

"All the problems in America are the result of people being led to believe things that are not true."
—Steven Jacobson, author and producer of the audio series
Mind Control in America and *Wake-Up America*

BIBLIOGRAPHY

ACLU. "New Documents Show FBI Targeting Environmental and Animal Rights Groups Activities as 'Domestic Terrorism.'" *ACLU. org*, December 20, 2005.

Adams, Jeanne. "I Am Many: Profiling the Ritual Abuse Survivor." *MKZine*, Winter 2004.

Albergotti, Reed. "Furor Erupts Over Facebook Experiment on Users." *The Wall Street Journal*, June 29, 2014.

Albrecht, Katherine, and Liz McIntyre. *SpyChips: How Major Coprorations and Government Plan to Track Your Every Purchase and Watch Your Every Move* (New York: Plume, 2004).

American Psychiatric Association. "The Diagnostic and Statistical Manual of Mental Disorders."

Ansary, Alex. "Mass Mind Control Through Network Television." Outside the Box, May, 29, 2012.

Arendt, Hannah. *Eichmann in Jerusalem: A Report on the Banality of Evil* (New York: Penguin Classics, 2006).

Bailey, GmB. *Closing the Gap: Gangstalking* (CreateSpace Independent Publishing, 2010).

Barker, Dr. Allen. "Motives for Mind Control." *MKZine*, Spring/Summer 2003.

Barrett, Dierdre. "The Psychological Power of Hypnosis." *Psychology Today*, January 2001.

Bell, Catherine. *Ritual: Perspectives and Dimensions* (New York: Oxford University Press, 1997).

———. *Ritual Theory, Ritual Practice* (New York: Oxford University Press, 2009).

Bergstein, Brian. "Despite Promise, Energy Bean Weapons Still Missing From Action." MSNBC.com, July 9, 2005.

Birns, H.D. *Hypnosis* (Award Books, 1968).

"Bizarre Cults." *Huffington Post*, September 6, 2013.

Braiker, Harriet B. *Who's Pulling Your Strings? How to Break the Cycle of Manipulation* (New York: McGraw Hill, 2004).

Brick, Neil. "How Cues and Programming Work in Mind Control and Propaganda." The Ritual Abuse, Secretive Organization and Mind Control Conference, Connecticut, May 24, 2003.

———. "Survivor Tactics." *MKZine*, Summer 2005.

———. "Ritual Abuse and its Political Implications." *MKZine*, Summer 2005.

Brzezinski, Zbignew. *Between Two Ages: America's Role in the Techno-tronic Era* (Praeger Publishing, 1982).

Chase, Alton. "Harvard and the Making of the Unabomber." *Atlantic Monthly*, June 2000.

Childs, Joe. "Sara's Choice: Scientology Clergy Force a Mother to Choose: Son or Daughter." *Tampa Bay Times*, March 2014.

Chopra, Deepak. "5 Steps to Harness the Power of Intention." *MindBodyGreen.com*, May 20, 2013. *www.mindbodygreen. com/0-9603/5-steps-to-harness-the-power-of-intention.html*.

Collins, Anne. *In the Sleep Room: The Story of CIA Brainwashing Experiments in Canada*, Reprint edition (Toronto, Canada: Key Porter Books, 1998).

Collins, Laura. "I Was a Queen of Scientology: President's Ex Wife Reveals the Church's Innermost Secrets and Why She Was Cast Into Darkness When She Finally Fled After 35 Years." *UK Daily Mail Online*, September 10–15, 2014.

Constantine, Alex. *Virtual Government: CIA Mind Control Operations in America* (Port Townsend, Wash.: Feral House, 1997).

Crump, Catherine, and Matthew Hardwood. "Big Brother Is Coming: Google, Mass Surveillance and the Rise of the Internet of Things." *Salon.com*, March 26, 2014.

Dober, Greg. "Experimentation on Prisoners: Persistent Dilemmas in Rights and Regulations." *Prison Legal News*, March 15, 2008.

Duncan, Robert. *Operation Soulcatcher: Secrets of Cyber and Cybernetic Warfare Revealed* (CreateSpace Independent Publishing, 2010).

Emery, Carla. *Secret, Don't Tell: The Encyclopedia of Hypnotism* (Pigeon Forge, Tenn.: Acorn Hill Publishing, 1997).

"Experimental Evidence of Massive Scale Emotional Contagion Through Social Networks," Proceedings of the National Academy of Sciences, Volume 111, Number 24.

Fields, R. Douglas. "The Power of Music: Mind Control by Rhythmic Sound." *Scientific American.com*, October 19, 2012.

Flemming, John. "The Menace of Satellite Surveillance." *EducateYourself. org*, June 19, 2003.

Freeland, Elana. "This Covert Electronic Era: Directed Energy Weapons for Political Control." Carnicorn Institute Webinar transcript, March 31, 2011.

_____. *Chemtrails, HAARP, and the Full Spectrum Dominance of Planet Earth* (Port Townsend, Wash.: Feral House, 2014).

Freeman, Jeremy, and Gary Marcus. *The Future of the Brain: Essays by the World's Leading Neuroscientists* (Princeton, N.J.: Princeton University Press, 2014).

Fulghum, David A. "Microwave Weapons May Be Ready for Iraq." *MK-Zine*, Spring/Summer 2003.

Gallagher, Ryan. "The Surveillance Engine: How the NSA Built its Own Secret Google." *FirstLook.org, The Intercept*, August 25, 2104.

Goodwin, Karin. "Brainwash Victims Win Cash Claims. *The Sunday Times*, October 17, 2004.

Hambling, David. "A Game of Tag: Implants and Electronic Harassment." *Fortean Times*, May 2011.

Hammond, Dr. Corydon. "Cults, Ritual Abuse and Mind Control: Exploring the Role of Cults in Ritual Abuse and Mind Control." *Wanttoknow.info.*

Hearst, Patricia Campbell, and Alvin Moscow. *Every Secret Thing* (New York: Doubleday, 1981).

Herrington, Boze. "The Seven Signs You're in a Cult." *The Atlantic Online*, June 18, 2014.

"High-Tech Psychological Warfare Arrives in the Middle East." ITV News Bureau Ltd. (London) news brief, March 23, 1991.

Hoffman, Michael A. *Secret Societies and Psychological Warfare* (Dresden, N.Y.: Wiswell Ruffin House, 1992).

Honor, Lenon. Website. *www.lenonhonor.com.*

Hunter, Edward. *Brainwashing* (New York: Pyramid Books, 1956).

"Hypnosis." New definition. Society of Psychological Hypnosis, Division 30, American Psychological Association.

Jacobsen, Annie. *Operation Paperclip: The Secret Intelligence Program That Brought Nazi Scientists to America* (New York: Little, Brown and Company, 2014).

Jacobson, Steven. *Mind Control in America.* CD audio program, MCiA Media, 2004–2014.

Janis, Irving. *Victims of Groupthink* (New York: Houghton Mifflin, 1972).

Johnson-Davis, Anne. *Hell Minus One: My Story of Deliverance From Satanic Ritual Abuse and My Journey to Freedom* (Transcript Bulletin Publishing, 2008).

Jones, Marie D., and Larry Flaxman. *The Grid: Exploring the Hidden Infrastructure of Reality* (San Antonio, Tex.: Hierophant Publishing, 2013).

Justesen, Dr. Don R. " Microwaves and Behavior." *American Psychologist 392* (March 1975): 391–401.

Karriker, W. "Torture-Based Mind Control as a Global Phenomenon," 13th International Conference on Violence, Abuse and Trauma, San Diego, California, September 2008.

Kurzweil, Ray. *The Singularity Is Near: When Humans Transcend Biology* (New York: Penguin Books, 2006).

Lammer, Dr. Helmut. *Milabs: Military Mind Control and Alien Abductions* (Illuminet Press, 1999).

Larry King Live. Guest Patty Hearst. CNN, January 22, 2002.

Leedom, Liane, MD. "Coercive Persuasion, Mind Control and Brainwashing." *Lovefraud.com*, August 31, 2007.

Leiser, Ken. "ACLU Study Warns of Unchecked Rise of Surveillance Cameras in St. Louis." *St. Louis Dispatch*, October 14, 2014.

Lifton, Robert J. *Thought Reform and the Psychology of Totalism* (University of North Carolina Press, July 1989).

MacMatzen, Morris. "Brain Hacking is Having Incredible Effects, and It's Just Getting Started." Yahoo.com Business Insider, August 16, 2014.

Madsen, Wayne. "James Holmes Family Tied to DARPA and Mind Manipulation Work." *Blacklisted News*, July 27, 2012.

Marks, John. *The Search for the "Manchurian Candidate": The CIA and Mind Control* (New York: Times Books, 1991).

McGowan, David. *Programmed to Kill: The Politics of Serial Murder* (iUniverse, 2004).

Monks, Kieron. "Spy Satellites Fight Crime From Space." CNNTech, August 12, 2014.

"Mystery Cults in the Greek and Roman World," Metropolitan Museum of Art Website. *www.metmuseum.org/toah/hd/myst/hd_myst.htm.*

Naylor, Gloria. *1996* (Chicago, Ill.: Third World Press, 2006).

Neighbors, Jacob. "Obey Your Father: Jim Jones' Rhetoric of Deadly Persuasion." San Diego State University, "Alternative Considerations of Jonestown and Peoples Temple," March 20, 2014.

Osmundsen, John A. "Matador With a Radio Stops Wired Bull." *New York Times*, July 9, 2014.

Pegues, Jeff. "NYPD: Threat of Terrorists With Drones Is a Growing Concern." New York CBSLocal.com, October 29, 2014.

Pehanick, Maggie. "Revolutionary Suicide: A Rhetorical Examination of Jim Jones' 'Death Tape.'" San Diego State University "Alternative Considerations of Jonestown and Peoples Temple."

Persinger, M.A. "On the Possibility of Directly Accessing Every Human Brain by Electromagnetic Induction of Fundamental Algorithms." *Perceptual and Motor Skills 80* (1995): 791.

Rath, Tom, and Donald O. Clifton, PhD. *How Full Is Your Bucket?* (New York: Gallup Press, 2004).

"The Reckoning: The Father of Sandy Hook Killer Searches for Answers." *The New Yorker*, March 17, 2014.

Redfern, Nick. *Close Encounters of the Fatal Kind* (Pompton Plains, N.J.: New Page Books, 2014).

Ross, Colin A. *The CIA Doctors: Human Rights Violations by American Pyschiatrists* (Richardson, Tex.: Manitou Communications, 2006).

Rutz, Carol. *A Nation Betrayed: The Chilling True Story of Secret Cold War Experiments on Our Children and Other Innocent People* (Grass Lake, Mich.: Fidelity Publishing, 2001).

———. "The Relevancy of Mind Control Today." *MKZine*, Winter/2003/2004.

Sample, Ian. "Neuroscience Could Mean Soldiers Controlling Weapons With Minds." *The Guardian* (UK), February 7, 2012.

Sasson, Remez. "The Power of Positive Thinking." *Successconciousness. com*, September 2014.

"Senate MKUltra Hearing: Appendix C—Documents Referring to Subprojects," page 167 (in PDF document page numbering). Senate Select Committee on Intelligence and Committee on Human Resources, August 3, 1977.

Shachtman, Noah. "Big Brother Gets a Brain." *Village Voice*, July 8, 2003.

Simon, George K. *In Sheep's Clothing: Understanding and Dealing With Manipulative People* (Chicago, Ill.: Parkhurst Brothers, 1996).

Singer, Dr. Margaret. "Coercive Mind Control Tactics." *F.A.C.T.Net.org*.

Streatfeild, Dominic. *Brainwash: The Secret History of Mind Control* (New York: Picador, 2008).

"Stunning Tale of Brainwashing, the CIA and an Unsuspecting Scots Researcher." *The Scotsman*, 2007.

Sullivan, Kathleen. *Unshackled: A Survivor's Story of Mind Control* (Dandelion Books, LLC, 2003).

Sweeney, H. Michael. *RFID, the TIAO, and the Mark of the Beast*, Third edition (The Professional Paranoid [*www.paranoidpress.com*], 2005).

Sweeney, H. Michael. "Your Cell Phone Is a Government Agent Spying on You." Blog post. ProParanoid, July 20, 2012.

Taylor, Eldon. *Mind Programming: From Persuasion and Brainwashing, to Self-Help and Practical Metaphysics* (Carlsbad, Calif.: Hay House, 2010).

Taylor, Kathleen. *Brainwashing: The Science of Thought Control* (New York: Oxford Press, 2006).

Thompson, Clive. "How to Keep the NSA Out of Your Computer." *Mother Jones Magazine*, August 2013.

Thomson, Helen. "Consciousness On-Off Switch Discovered Deep in Brain." *New Scientist*, July 2, 2014.

Thorn, Victor. *Conspireality* (Stafford, Va.: Life and Liberty Publishing, 2013).

Timberg, Craig. "New Surveillance Technology Can Track Everyone in an Area for Several Hours at a Time." *Washington Post*, February 5, 2014.

Vincent, James. "Mass Surveillance of UK Citizens on Facebook, YouTube and Google is Legal, Says Official." *The Independent* (UK), June 17, 2014.

Wall, Judy. "Mind Control With Silent Sounds and Super Computers." *Nexus Magazine*, October/November 1998.

Waugh, Evelyn. *The Ordeal of Gilbert Pinfold* (New York: Back Bay Books, a division of Hachette, 2012).

Weinberger, Sharon. "Mind Games." *Washington Post*, January 14, 2007.

West, Nicholas. "7 Future Methods of Mind Control." *Activist Post*, July 1, 2013.

———. "Mind Control Scientists Claim Ability to Turn Off Consciousness." *The Sleuth Journal*, July 11, 2014.

Zimbardo, Dr. Philip G. "Mind Control: Psychological Reality or Mindless Rhetoric?" *APA.org*, November 2002.

Index

ABOUT THE AUTHORS

Marie D. Jones

Marie D. Jones is the best-selling author of *Destiny vs. Choice: The Scientific and Spiritual Evidence Behind Fate and Free Will; 2013: End of Days or a New Beginning—Envisioning the World After the Events of 2012; PSIence: How New Discoveries in Quantum Physics and New Science May Explain the Existence of Paranormal Phenomena*; and *Looking for God in All the Wrong Places*. Marie co-authored with her father, geophysicist Dr. John Savino, *Supervolcano: The Catastrophic Event That Changed the Course of Human History*. She is also the co-author of *11:11—The Time Prompt Phenomenon: The Meaning Behind Mysterious Signs, Sequences, and Synchronicities; The Resonance Key: Exploring the Links Between Vibration, Consciousness, and the Zero Point Grid; The Déjà vu Enigma: A Journey Through the Anomalies of Mind, Memory, and Time*; and *The Trinity Secret: The Power of Three and the Code of Creation* with Larry Flaxman, her partner in ParaExplorers.com, an organization devoted to exploring unknown mysteries. Before this, their latest book was *This*

Book Is From the Future: A Journey Through Portals, Relativity, Wormholes, and Other Adventures in Time Travel. Marie and Larry have also launched the ParaExplorer Series of eBooks and articles introducing readers to a variety of subjects.

Marie has an extensive background in metaphysics, cutting-edge science, and the paranormal, and has worked as a field investigator for MUFON (Mutual UFO Network) in Los Angeles and San Diego in the 1980s and 1990s. She currently serves as a consultant and director of special projects for ARPAST, the Arkansas Paranormal and Anomalous Studies Team, where she works with ARPAST president Larry Flaxman to develop theories that can test in the field. Marie is a former licensed New Thought/Metaphysics minister and has trained extensively in the Science of Mind/New Thought arena.

Marie has been on television, most recently on the History Channel's *Nostradamus Effect* series and Ancient Aliens series, and served as a special UFO/abduction consultant for the 2009 Universal Pictures science fiction movie *The Fourth Kind.* She has been interviewed on hundreds of radio talk shows all over the world, including Coast to Coast AM, NPR, KPBS Radio, Dreamland, the X-Zone, Kevin Smith Show, Paranormal Podcast, Cut to the Chase, Feet 2 the Fire, World of the Unexplained, and the Shirley MacLaine Show, and has been featured in dozens of newspapers, magazines, and online publications all over the world. She is a staff writer and official blogger for *Intrepid Magazine,* and a regular contributor to *New Dawn Magazine,* and her essays and articles have appeared in *TAPS ParaMagazine, Phenomena, Whole Life Times, Light Connection, Vision, Conspiracy Journal, Beyond Reality,* and several popular anthologies, such as *If Women Ruled the World, Let Go! And Let Miracles Happen,* three *Hot Chocolate for the Soul* books, and five *Chicken Soup for the Soul* books. She has also contributed and co-authored more than 50 inspirational books for New Seasons/PIL.

She has lectured widely at major metaphysical, paranormal, new science, and self-empowerment events, including "Through the Veil," "Queen Mary Weekends," "TAPS Academy Training," "CPAK," and "Paradigm Symposium," "Conscious Expo," and "Darkness Radio Events," and is a popular public speaker on the subjects of cutting-edge science, the paranormal, metaphysics, Noetics, and human potential. She speaks often at local metaphysical centers, churches, local libraries, bookstore signings, film festivals, and regional meet-ups on writing, the paranormal, human consciousness, science, and metaphysical subjects.

She is also the screenwriter and co-producer of *19 Hz*, a paranormal thriller, as well as a science fiction feature film titled *Aurora*, and she serves as a co-host on the popular Dreamland Radio Show.

Marie has also released her first of many novels, *EKHO—Evil Kid Hunting Organization*, written with her son, Max, and has a YA paranormal thriller, *FREAK*, and a sci-fi conspiracy thriller, *Black Mariah*, coming out in 2015. She also has a novel with Larry Flaxman titled *Gridwalkers* releasing in 2016.

Larry Flaxman

Larry Flaxman is the best-selling author of *11:11—The Time Prompt Phenomenon: The Meaning Behind Mysterious Signs, Sequences, and Synchronicities; The Resonance Key: Exploring the Links Between Vibration, Consciousness, and the Zero Point Grid; The Déjà vu Enigma: A Journey Through the Anomalies of Mind, Memory, and Time;* and *The Trinity Secret: The Power of Three and the Code of Creation* with Marie D. Jones, his partner in ParaExplorers.com. Prior to this release, his latest book was *This Book Is From the Future: A Journey Through Portals, Relativity, Wormholes, and Other Adventures in Time Travel*.

Larry has been actively involved in paranormal research and hands-on field investigation for more than 13 years, and melds his technical, scientific, and investigative backgrounds together for no-nonsense, scientifically objective explanations regarding a variety of anomalous phenomena. He is the president and senior researcher of ARPAST, the Arkansas Paranormal and Anomalous Studies Team, which he founded in February 2007. Under his leadership, ARPAST has become one of the nation's largest and most active paranormal research organizations, with more than 150 members worldwide. Widely respected for his expertise on the proper use of equipment and techniques for conducting a solid investigation, Larry also serves as technical advisor to several paranormal research groups throughout the country.

Larry has appeared on Discovery Channel's *Ghost Lab* and History Channel's *Ancient Aliens* series, and has been interviewed for dozens of print and online publications, including *The Anomalist, Times Herald News, Jacksonville Patriot, ParaWeb, Current Affairs Herald, Unexplained Magazine, The Petit Jean County Headlight, the Villager Online,* and *The Pine Bluff Commercial.* He has appeared on hundreds of radio programs all over the world, including Coast to Coast with George Noory, TAPS Family Radio, Encounters Radio, Higher Dimensions, X-Zone, Ghostly Talk, Eerie Radio, Crossroads Paranormal, Binall of America, World of the Unexplained, and Haunted Voices.

Larry is a staff writer and official blogger for *Intrepid Magazine,* and his work has appeared regularly in *TAPS ParaMagazine, New Dawn Magazine,* and *Phenomena.* He is also a screenwriter of a paranormal thriller, *19 Hz,* and a popular public speaker, lecturing widely at paranormal and metaphysical conferences and events all over the country, including major appearances at "Through the Veil," "History, Haunts and Legends," "Paradigm Symposium," "ESP Weekend at the Crescent Hotel," "The Texas GhostShow," and "DragonCon." He also speaks widely at local and regional meet-ups, bookstore signings, libraries, and events on the subjects of science, the paranormal, metaphysics, Noetics, and human potential. Larry is also active in the development of cutting-edge, custom-designed equipment for use in the field investigating environmental effects and anomalies that may contribute to our understanding of the paranormal.

Larry has his first novel releasing in 2016, titled *Gridwalkers,* based in part upon the scientific theory and research in his non-fiction book with Marie D. Jones, *The Grid.*